A Study Skills Survival Guide for Neurodivergent Learners

A Pick-and-Mix of Study Skills Strategies for ADHD, Autistic, Dyslexic and Dyspraxic Learners

JULIA CHILDS

Illustrated by Jules Scheele

Jessica Kingsley Publishers
London and Philadelphia

First published in Great Britain in 2025 by Jessica Kingsley Publishers
An imprint of John Murray Press

1

Copyright © Julia Childs 2025
Illustration copyright © Jules Scheele 2025

The right of Julia Childs to be identified as the Author of the Work has been asserted by her in accordance with the Copyright, Designs and Patents Act 1988.

Front cover image source: Shutterstock®. The cover image is for illustrative purposes only, and any person featuring is a model.

All rights reserved. No part of this publication may be reproduced, stored in a retrieval system, or transmitted, in any form or by any means without the prior written permission of the publisher, nor be otherwise circulated in any form of binding or cover other than that in which it is published and without a similar condition being imposed on the subsequent purchaser.

All pages marked with 📖 can be downloaded for personal use with this programme, but may not be reproduced for any other purposes without the permission of the publisher.

A CIP catalogue record for this title is available from the British Library and the Library of Congress

ISBN 978 1 80501 185 9
eISBN 978 1 80501 186 6

Printed and bound in Great Britain by Ashford Colour Ltd

Jessica Kingsley Publishers' policy is to use papers that are natural, renewable and recyclable products and made from wood grown in sustainable forests. The logging and manufacturing processes are expected to conform to the environmental regulations of the country of origin.

Jessica Kingsley Publishers
Carmelite House
50 Victoria Embankment
London EC4Y 0DZ

www.jkp.com

John Murray Press
Part of Hodder & Stoughton Ltd
An Hachette Company

The authorised representative in the EEA is Hachette Ireland, 8 Castlecourt Centre, Dublin 15, D15 XTP3, Ireland (email: info@hbgi.ie)

of related interest

The Memory and Processing Guide for Neurodiverse Learners
Strategies for Success
Alison Patrick
Illustrated by Matthew Patrick
ISBN 978 1 78775 072 2
eISBN 978 1 78775 073 9

The Dyslexia, ADHD, and DCD-Friendly Study Skills Guide
Tips and Strategies for Exam Success
Ann-Marie McNicholas
ISBN 978 1 78775 177 4
eISBN 978 1 80501 513 0

The Procrastination Playbook for Adults with ADHD
How to Catch Sneaky Forms of Procrastination Before They Catch You
Risa Williams
ISBN 978 1 80501 229 0
eISBN 978 1 80501 230 6

The Young Person's Guide to Autistic Burnout
Viv Dawes
Illustrated by Josh Dawes
ISBN 978 1 80501 732 5
eISBN 978 1 80501 733 2

CONTENTS

Introduction — 7

1. How We Learn — 19
2. Self-Care: Avoiding Overwhelm and Burnout — 27
3. Getting Organized — 61
4. Overcoming Barriers to Learning: Avoiding Procrastination — 91
5. Managing in Class and Note-taking in Lectures — 105
6. Reading and Understanding Source Material — 119
7. Completing Assignments, Essays and Dissertations — 143
8. Achieving Your Goals in Exams — 207
9. Oral Skills — 237

Conclusion — 244
Useful Sources — 245
Glossary — 247
Endnotes — 253

INTRODUCTION

This guide is the result of many hours working with neurodivergent students, supporting them to successfully navigate their way through school, college and university. During this time, I have found that study skills advice is often grouped specifically and individually for autism, dyslexia, ADHD (attention deficit hyperactivity disorder) and other neurodivergent conditions, whereas my practical experience is that these often overlap and co-occur. This means that common approaches to study skills which pigeonhole students according to a single diagnosed condition can sometimes feel too constraining and impractical.

One thing that neurodivergent students almost always have in common is having a so-called 'spiky profile', which means that they excel in some areas and are less strong in others rather than being considered 'all-rounders' (whatever that means). In general terms, I have also found that neurodivergent students are often able to think very broadly about a problem or a topic, which results in interesting ideas and creative problem-solving.

I hope to support you in the development of your study skills so that you can become more aware of what works for you and what you need help with. That way we can help you to play on your strengths (the top of those spikes) while being realistic about some of the challenges you face.

What's inside?

I have provided a 'pick-and-mix' selection of strategies, which acknowledges that one size does not fit all and you can, and should, experiment. The focus is on giving you practical strategies to add to your study skills bag. In each section, you will find a range of different ideas. My advice would be to try the strategies which instinctively appeal most to you first. With luck, they will be immediately successful; however, if something doesn't feel right or isn't helping, then just move on to try something different.

It is well worth taking some time to experiment with different ideas because once you find something that works, it's a strategy that you can use forever. Many of these tips can be usefully applied in life outside of academic studies, particularly those which relate to personal organization and time management.

I have used some icons to represent different ideas which I hope will make navigating your way around this book a bit easier. Here's a key:

Key to icons

 Indicates quick tips, spread throughout the chapters.

 Downloadable templates of some of the tables in this book can be found at www.jkp.com/catalogue/book/9781805011859 for your own use, as indicated when you see this icon.

 A quick recap list of areas covered at the end of each chapter. It works a bit like a mini-contents list, so you can use it to see what's in a chapter at a glance.

 A list of key takeaway points which you will find at the end of each chapter.

What else?

I am very aware of this phrase which is often used by disability rights campaigners: 'Nothing about us, without us.'[1] This is the idea that people should be fully involved in any decisions, proposals or policies which affect them. I know that neurodivergent people can often feel that they are on the receiving end of advice rather than being involved in the giving of advice. This is one of the reasons that I have included some case studies where I have used anonymized examples from my experience of working with neurodivergent students over the years. I hope that these will demonstrate how the practical strategies provided work in real life.

I would also like to sincerely thank the students I work with. They are generous in sharing their ideas and challenges. This helps me to learn more every day and I try to pass this on so I can improve the way that I support other students. They have also made me increasingly aware of my own different ways of thinking! I come from a very neurodivergent family, so it would hardly be surprising if I am also part of the community.

Before we get down to the details, I think it is worth pausing for a moment to define what I mean by some of the key phrases I'll use in this book.

*Do you feel like you already know which areas you want to focus on? If so, you could skip straight ahead to the section that appeals to you most. This **is** a pick-and-mix book of strategies!*

Key terms and definitions

Study skills

This little phrase is a handy term to describe the huge range of strategies, techniques and methods that we can use to help us learn most effectively. Developing strong study skills, which are individually tailored, can improve your capacity to organize your studies and retain and recall information.

Executive function

This term is used to describe a set of cognitive factors that help people to plan, manage and achieve their goals. These include mental skills related to attention, working memory, inhibition and problem-solving.[2] If you have differences in executive functioning it can make things like personal organization tricky, which can have a knock-on effect on your ability to do as well as you would like in your studies.[3]

Neurodiversity

Neurodiversity[4] is a way to describe a **group** of people. The term is based on the idea that there are natural variations in ways of thinking and processing. That means that any community will be neurodiverse in nature and will include a mixture of neurodivergent and neurotypical people. People within this community will have unique skills, abilities and needs.

Neurodivergent

This term was coined by Kassiane Asasumasu[5] as a non-medical way of describing **a person** whose thinking differs from that which might otherwise be considered 'typical'. It's useful because it is a single word that can encompass many different ways of thinking, so it allows for the fact that neurodivergent conditions overlap.

Conditions generally considered to be neurodivergent and considered in this book include:

- autism
- ADHD
- dyslexia
- dyscalculia
- dysgraphia
- developmental coordination disorder (DCD), also known as dyspraxia
- Tourette's and other conditions which cause tics.

Sometimes, other conditions such as acquired neurodivergence (like those caused by brain injury), learning difficulties and mental health conditions are also included in this 'list'. Apart from considering the importance of mental health needs, these other areas aren't discussed in this guide, though some of the suggested strategies might be helpful.

Neurotypical

This describes a person (or a group of people) who is not neurodivergent. So, they are 'typical' compared to others. We could debate what 'typical' actually means, or whether anyone is really 'typical' at all!

Some general comments about terminology

As a relatively recent invention, the use of the word neurodivergent (or neurodivergence) is not without criticism. Terminology within these communities is controversial and evolving. Its use in this book is in no way intended to diminish or to detract from individual identities, nor to minimize some of the difficulties that students with particular types of learning differences can face.

My use of 'neurodivergent' as an umbrella term has mainly been for practical reasons. It would be beyond boring if I listed every kind of condition which might work with each strategy. That said, I will sometimes mention a specific neurodivergent profile where I feel a strategy is particularly geared towards this. You will find some more definitions of terminology scattered throughout, as well as a useful glossary at the end of this book.

I will also briefly cover some of the physical and emotional difficulties students can face, simply because we need to be thinking about you as a 'whole' person, not as the sum of your constituent parts! However, I am not medically trained, so I need to say that if any of these issues are particularly challenging for you, I strongly advise you to seek professional advice.

A note about artificial intelligence (AI)

The use of AI within academic writing is very much a contested and developing area. There are times when I suggest it might be a useful tool for you to try.

However, I caution you to always check your educational institution's policy thoroughly **before** you do so. Some may ban its use altogether, and if that applies to you, please comply with this or you will face the threat of being accused of plagiarism which can have very serious consequences indeed.

I would add that AI is also fallible and can produce output which is of dubious quality. So, it can never replace your own critical thinking skills. Something else you might like to consider is the environmental impact of the use of AI. There are increasing concerns about the amount of energy required to run such large systems.[6]

How to use this book

This book is designed for you to be able to dip in and out as you see fit. You don't need to read it from front to back or cover to cover. Again, the key thing to remember is that one size does not fit all! You are going to need to experiment with different ideas and strategies to find something that works for you. Remember too that you might need to try different approaches between subjects. So, one method might work well for you in one scenario but not in another. That can be a bit frustrating, but it's quite usual. For example, a note-taking method you use effectively in a class on medical history (text heavy) might not work so well in a class on pharmacology (maths heavy).

I've given you many ideas to choose from and that means you can use this book in a variety of different ways. You could try the following:

* Go straight to the chapter which covers the areas you find most tricky. That works best if you already know what you'd like to learn more about.

* Read the final page of each chapter first. This is where you'll find a list of key points covered and the main takeaway ideas. If you are not quite sure where you need most support this will help you to decide whether it's relevant to you.

* Flick through and look for the lightbulb icons – these are the quick tips. This is a good approach if you aren't strongly motivated to read. It might trigger a bit of an 'aha!' feeling and stimulate your interest.

* Make notes in the margin of the book so you can remember which strategies you've tried and which work best.

Here's a quick summary of the chapters, which might help you to decide which ones you would like to read first.

Summary of chapters

1. **How We Learn**

   This is a good place to start if you would like to have an understanding of some underpinning ideas around memory and learning. It includes information on working memory and explains why this is key when you are studying. It also discusses the role of learning about learning (metacognition) and the importance of trying to decrease your cognitive load, and so reduce any feelings of overwhelm.

2. **Self-Care: Avoiding Overwhelm and Burnout**

   Enjoying your learning is important and that means that keeping mentally and physically well is vital. If that's something you find tricky, you might like to read about some of the common experiences of other students and have some strategies to help you avoid running out of energy or feeling overwhelmed. There's also some information on playing to your strengths and on remembering the importance of food, exercise and sleep. It finishes with some tips for disclosing your neurodivergence and becoming more confident with self-advocacy.

3. **Getting Organized**

   This chapter is mainly about sorting! There are **lots** of ideas about different ways you can organize your space, time and things. It explains the importance of having a routine and rhythm but fully acknowledges that a rigid structure might be the opposite of what some of you need. That means it gives a variety of time management strategies for you to try out. It also includes some prioritization techniques and ideas that might help if you tend to lose yourself or your things. Quite a few of the ideas in this section will be useful for life outside of studying and can be taken forward into your future.

4. **Overcoming Barriers to Learning: Avoiding Procrastination**

   It's not always easy to get started with a task and this is where you can find many tips and strategies to help you when you are feeling 'stuck'. There's also a section on maintaining focus more generally when you are studying, and on getting back on track if you find your mind wandering.

5. **Managing in Class and Note-taking in Lectures**

   Studying by ourselves is one thing, but working alongside or with others brings its own set of challenges. This chapter contains a list of strategies for maintaining focus and reducing overwhelm in class before moving on to look at how you can take effective notes. There are nine different note-taking ideas for you to try here!

6. **Reading and Understanding Source Material**

   In this chapter, we discuss some important underpinning reading skills. It explains how you can use these skills to help you fully understand reading material so that you can grasp concepts and apply your knowledge. There are three different reading strategies to try out and some ideas about how you could use technology to help.

7. **Completing Assignments, Essays and Dissertations**

   Writing can be quite a complicated process! Here, each stage is broken down into smaller steps so that it's easier to understand what we need to do. You will find advice around using feedback to improve your work, how to understand questions and how to select information to include. Common structures for writing are explained, together with lots of different ideas about how to plan your writing. It can also be tricky to decide what style and tone of language to use, so there's a section on that too. Something that students often find hard is making sure they have a solid, well-evidenced argument running through their work – you will find some tips and strategies to help you with this. This can be particularly challenging if you are working in a group – so there are some suggestions about how to deal with the common problems here. Finally, you will find some tips for referencing and proofreading.

8. **Achieving Your Goals in Exams**

   Exams are always stressful and it's important to remember that your health and wellbeing always come first. So, the main aim of this chapter is to reduce some of the stress around this by helping you to feel fully prepared. There are lots of different revision strategies to try, as well as some ideas about how you can manage both your time and your feelings when you are doing an exam.

9. **Oral Skills**

   Having to speak in front of people can be nerve-wracking, but it's something that is required in lots of courses. This chapter focuses on how to structure and prepare for presentations and spoken examinations. It includes some tips for reducing anxiety and making sure you have the support you need in place.

So, the overall aim here is to enable you to become a more successful, independent student. I do hope this guide is useful and interesting, and that some of the strategies help you achieve the very best of your unique abilities.

Let's recap

In this chapter we have covered:

- what's inside this book
- key definitions
- comments on terminology
- a note about AI.

 Key takeaway points from this chapter

- This is a pick-and-mix book.
- Flick through and focus on the chapters/areas which are most relevant for you.
- Try out different strategies until you find ones that suit you best.

Chapter 1

HOW WE LEARN

Research[1] tells us that it is very helpful for **all** students to have a basic grasp of how learning and memory work. That's particularly important if you are neurodivergent because issues with working memory have been included in almost every diagnostic assessment I have ever read.

> *Working memory temporarily holds new information so that we can work with it to make connections or perform tasks, for example, taking two numbers and adding them together.*

So, as the next few chapters are very much about the nuts and bolts of day-to-day studying, I think it is worth taking some time to talk about how we learn. I will add that memory is complex and there are lots of different ideas about how it works! This is just an overview which is designed to give you a taste of things.

From the beginning I should tell you that memory doesn't work the same way as a computer, even though that's a comparison which is often made. We do not simply store and retrieve data because we make sense of information by **relating** it to pre-existing knowledge and through making associations. That means we can help our memories by looking for these links and by making them explicit. Lots of the study ideas discussed later are designed to exploit this way of learning.

If we accept that brains are not computers then it's not surprising that memory can be unreliable, inaccurate or incomplete! That's because all learning takes place within a wider setting, and this impacts how memories are made and retrieved. Let's look at an example:

> ### How memory might work in context
>
> Imagine that yesterday you were taught by two different tutors.
>
> - Farida speaks clearly and has well-organized slides.
> - Julie has a dull voice and her slides can be difficult to understand.
> - Which content do you think you might remember the most easily?
>
> I suspect most of you will have said that Farida's lecture is most likely to be recalled better.
>
> Now, let's think about the effect the passage of time might have on our learning and memory. Imagine Farida's clear lecture took place nine months ago and Julie's dull lecture took place today.
>
> - Which one will you remember better now?
> - Has that changed your answer?

All of this means that **how** and **when** we retrieve the information from our memories makes a difference in terms of how **accurately** and **easily** we can recall it. You will find more about this in Chapter 8, which discusses preparing for exams.

Working memory systems

Let's have a quick look at a simplified diagram of our working memory system[2] so that we can understand what this means in practice:

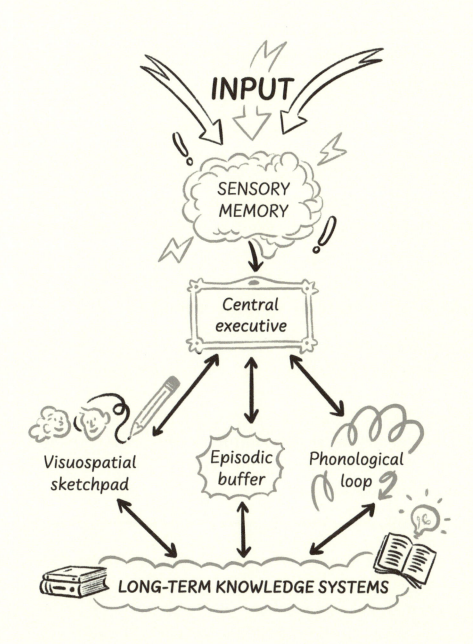

I'm going to explain each of these components in turn just to give you a feel of how things can work. Please remember though that this is a very simplified version of things! There is a lot of information about memory online, so I would encourage you to go and explore if it's something you are interested in.

The central executive

The 'boss' of your memory is the central executive. You can think of it sitting in the middle of your memory system, like a conductor on a podium, organizing activities and making sure that things run smoothly.

We don't need to hold on to every piece of information that enters our memory systems, so the central executive also decides what is important and what is not. It helps us to filter out anything we don't need, and to transfer other information into our long-term knowledge systems. Some information just decays over time, too, and we will forget it if we don't regularly remind ourselves about it.

An example of the role of working memory

I smell garlic cooking as I walk down the street. That sensory input is noted by my central executive. That might be unimportant, so it is 'thrown out' of my memory system. Alternatively, it may remind me I've forgotten to book a table for my friends at our favourite pizzeria! Now I need to 'hold on to' that memory so that I can perform further actions. I must use my working memory skills to call the restaurant, message my friends, choose how to get there and decide what to wear.

Looking at that example, you can see that the central executive has an important role in directing our attention. It's why you may hear people say they have 'executive functioning failure' when they have forgotten to do something. Differences in executive functioning can cause real challenges in day-to-day life, particularly when it comes to managing school, college or university life. It's something that comes up **a lot** for neurodivergent students. There are some practical tips for helping you to remember equipment and other items later in this book (see 'Organizing your other stuff' in Chapter 3 'Getting Organized').

Phonological loop, episodic buffer and visuospatial sketch pad

Let's move on to talk about the role of the three areas, which sit between the central executive and the long-term knowledge systems, as they play a vital role here too.

While they all have different jobs to do, they are all continuously working together to process inputs:

1. **The phonological loop** is concerned with the manipulation and storage of sound, i.e. spoken word. It holds words that we hear, and also processes sound so that we can articulate, both internally (things like repeating information to ourselves to remember it) and externally (speaking).

   If we have issues with phonological processing, it can have a big impact on reading and writing (not only speaking), as we might not be able to sound out words or distinguish between similar sounds clearly. Students who can't hear the subtle differences between some alphabet sounds are sometimes told they have difficulties with auditory discrimination. That's particularly common in dyslexia.

   > *'Phono' comes from Greek, meaning sound/voice. Think of the word: tele**phone**.*

2. **The episodic buffer** is important to help us maintain a sense of time and sequencing. It acts by pulling together and combining information from the other components, and putting this into some kind of order (or chronology). Sometimes students find sequencing very difficult; for example, they may have found learning the order of the alphabet or telling the time very tricky as children.

3. **The visuospatial sketchpad** is responsible for manipulating and storing visual information. This helps us to make sense of the world and also helps us to be able to link shapes with meaning. For example, sounds are represented by symbols in languages (think about the shapes of the letters of the alphabet). It also has an important role in helping us to find our way around. To navigate, we

need to be able to understand the spatial environment and to recognize visual characteristics of people, places and things.

Long-term knowledge systems

Sometimes we need to embed information more permanently, both for studying and for life skills; think of things like remembering your credit card PIN! This is where we need to use our long-term knowledge systems which 'sit' at the bottom of the model. The research[3] tells us that using a variety of actively different methods, which are spaced over some time, works best in terms of helping longer-term recall. Practice and repetition are very much the key here as these help to prevent the decay of information which naturally happens over time.

> ### An example of using longer-term memory systems
>
> We can use the example of that credit card PIN again here. We used to have to physically input our PIN every time we bought something. For most people, that made remembering that number pretty effortless because it was retrieved so regularly in lots of different environments. Now, many of us mainly use contactless payment, so when we do need to use our PIN, we have to think about it. That's because that regular recall isn't happening any more.

It is important to understand that **multiple** processes are happening simultaneously within this system (look at the arrows on the diagram to see what I mean), and that is why sometimes it can feel a bit overwhelming if there is lots of incoming information in a short space of time.

You may have read that very quick overview of our memory systems and recognized some of the areas that you find harder or easier for you. If so, you can use this information to help you work out which study strategies work best for you, particularly if you are actively thinking about the effectiveness of the strategy when you are trying it out. That's where metacognition comes in.

Metacognition

Metacognition is a vital skill that you can use whenever you are studying. It just means being aware of the process of learning **in that moment**, so it's not quite the same thing as reflection (which is covered later in this book).

So, while you are trying out one of the strategies I suggest later on, ask yourself some questions:

* How does this feel?

* Am I getting done what I need to? Why? How?

* How is this different to what I've done before? How? Why?

You can also use metacognition to help you recognize which situations cause you the most difficulty in terms of taking in new information. This helps you to work out what causes you **cognitive overload**. The next step is to try to reduce that cognitive load.

> *Cognitive overload happens when your memory is trying to hold and process too much at once — when the amount of incoming information exceeds your capacity.*

This process of thinking about your learning is always useful, even if you find out that you hate using a particular study skill technique! It helps you decide the kind of strategy you might like to try next. This should also allow you to develop a more accurate perception of your own independent study skills. Being able to develop **sustainable** study skills practice is vital and leads me to the next chapter.

Let's recap

In this chapter we have covered:

- an explanation of working memory and its parts:
  - central executive (executive functioning)
  - phonological loop, episodic buffer, visuospatial sketchpad
  - long-term knowledge systems
- metacognition
- cognitive overload.

 Key takeaway points from this chapter

- Thinking about how you learn can really help you develop excellent study skills.

- You will remember things better if you can make mental links or associations between ideas.

- Mix things up if you are revising, and try to recall information regularly and often so that your knowledge doesn't 'decay'.

Chapter 2

SELF-CARE

Avoiding Overwhelm and Burnout

Introduction

This chapter is deliberately placed near the start of this book even though you might not think it is directly related to study skills. That's because you can't study effectively and perform to the very best of your abilities if you are not taking care of yourself.[1]

There is also quite a bit of research[2] which shows us the kind of steps that students can take to improve their own feelings of happiness. The trouble is that this research doesn't necessarily differentiate between neurotypical and neurodivergent students. That means that some of the advice, such as striking up conversations with strangers, might well have the reverse effect on wellbeing for some students who find social interaction particularly challenging! However, it **does** tell us that paying attention to your own happiness regularly and consciously can help you to feel more consistently happy. That's definitely something useful to keep in mind.

I feel **very** strongly about the importance of keeping the joy of learning. I've noticed that very many neurodivergent students choose their subjects because of a deeply felt interest and sense of enjoyment. It saddens me to see some students lose this because of study-related stress and that's a key reason why I decided to write this book. This means that establishing **sustainable** study practices is vital. This can be a particular challenge as you might have differences which make you more susceptible to so-called 'overwhelm', 'overload' and 'burnout', where it just becomes impossible to keep going.

Overwhelm

> **Overwhelm** is when things just get too much and there are lots of causes. Sometimes this can lead to a **shutdown** or a **meltdown**.

Overwhelm is a stress response. There are many causes which are often combined, but generally, it's a sign that you may be struggling to process 'incoming' information. That might happen if you are on the receiving end of too much written or spoken information which is causing cognitive overload. Equally, it might be the result of feeling overwhelmed by the amount of social interaction that is required, or by an unexpected change of events.

Sensory overload is another very common cause of overwhelm, particularly if you are someone with sensory processing differences. If there is too much sensory input to process, it can feel very uncomfortable indeed. For example, you might become overwhelmed at a loud party that is packed with unfamiliar people and where there is no air conditioning. This can also happen when there is too much emotional input, and this doesn't necessarily need to be 'negative' input. It could be a huge amount of attention given to you on your birthday.

Feeling overwhelmed can result in meltdowns or shutdowns. These are terms that are most often associated with autistic and ADHD people, but they are also experienced by those with other neurodivergent conditions.

A meltdown results in potentially losing the ability to regulate your emotions, leading to strong emotional behaviour such as crying, agitation or outbursts. A shutdown can feel a bit like you have gone into 'standby' mode. Everything switches off. You might be unable to communicate or move. Students tell me that both of these states are horrible to experience, and many worry about what others will think of them.

Burnout and masking

> **Burnout** *is when a person is so mentally and physically exhausted that they can no longer manage day-to-day activities or social interactions.*

'Burnout' can be experienced by everyone and there are different kinds of burnout too; however, here we are talking about neurodivergent burnout. It's a term most often used to explain the experiences of some autistic and ADHD people. That's because burnout is caused by environments not being suitable for them, feeling drained and exhausted from masking or experiencing too much sensory input.

> **Masking or camouflaging** *is a phrase which is often used, particularly by people in the autistic community, to describe how they have learned that they must appear to be neurotypical in social situations (like school) to 'fit in' better.*

Sometimes masking is deliberate and sometimes it becomes a more subconsciously learned behaviour. Some students tell me that they have masked for so long, that it's not always easy for them to know when they are doing it and when they aren't. Whichever the case, this means they are 'pushing down', or hiding their natural way of being.

Masking is usually the result of having experienced negative reactions when you **have** behaved in ways which are entirely natural for you. One example might be a natural tendency to stim when you're excited or happy. Stimming is the word we use to describe repeated movements or sounds. A child might stim by spinning or flapping their hands. In this example, it would help them to express pleasure and would feel nice for them. If they are repeatedly told not to do this by adults, or laughed at by their peers, they are quite likely to try to suppress these behaviours. Eye contact is another example. An autistic person might find eye contact very uncomfortable but has learned that this is expected behaviour in some situations, so they might force themselves to do it.

There are too many examples for me to include here, but it is reasonable to assume that having to continually monitor yourself, observe those around you and constantly adjust your behaviour to conform to a way that is considered more 'socially acceptable' is exhausting. It can also be anxiety inducing as students tell me there is the fear that they will 'get it wrong'. This is one reason that social interaction can be so tiring and overwhelming for some neurodivergent people. It can certainly contribute to feelings of burnout.

> **A caveat**: It is best not to assume that all autistic people (or those with other kinds of neurodivergence) mask! I have worked with many students who do, but it is not universal. This is just something to bear in mind when you are looking at designing sustainable study practices for yourself, particularly factoring in the level of tiredness you might feel after social interaction.

So, we can see that **burnout is a status that happens as a result of a sustained period of stress**. It's often considered to be the result of prolonged periods of having to be 'fully functioning' in a neurotypical world, which can be incredibly wearing, regardless of whether someone is masking or not.

My firm advice to you is to think about these things while you are feeling relatively stress-free because, by the time you reach a state where you are already overwhelmed or burnt out, it can be impossible to put supporting strategies in place for yourself.

Remember, we don't want you to get to the point of being overwhelmed, let alone to the stage of burnout! So, let's look at some common challenges faced by students and then some ways to deal with them.

 Are you finding this a bit stressful to read? Would you like to skip straight to the tips rather than being reminded about the things that you find tricky? Then you can go straight to the section in this chapter: 'Strategies for preventing and combatting overwhelm'.

Some common experiences

Despite the hugely individual nature of neurodivergent conditions, there are some common experiences that students have shared with me. Have a look at the speech bubbles below and think about whether any of these relate to you.

Monotropism and hyper-focus

Do you sometimes become absorbed in a subject or activity to the exclusion of everything else?

You might have heard this called monotropism or hyper-focus. Sometimes, particularly for autistic students, this can be framed as being a so-called 'special interest'. Other students explain how they experience a kind of tunnel vision when they are so intensely focused that everything else becomes unimportant (some of my students with ADHD have mentioned this). They might also feel this as a deep emotional connection to the subject or activity.

This can be a distinct advantage when it comes to exploring an issue or subject. Looking back with our modern lens, we think that many of the world's greatest discoveries and valuable insights have been provided by neurodivergent folks.[3] However, there can be a flipside to this tendency. It means that you might neglect areas of your life which feel peripheral when you are in a hyper-focused state. This might include your basic needs like remembering to eat, drink or shower.

Executive function – challenges with planning and time management

Do you experience time differently?

I have met many students who say that time has a very different 'feel' for them. Some describe how it passes more slowly or quickly depending upon the activity, time of the day, month or year. Others say that time doesn't feel linear at all and that it is more circular. This is one of the reasons that I enjoy working with neurodivergent students so much – everyone is unique.

In research, differences in the perception of time are something which has been described mainly in young people with ADHD,[4] with studies showing difficulties estimating time. This can be challenging if you are trying to get to class promptly, do revision or meet deadlines. If this is coupled with a tendency toward hyper-focus, it can help explain why some students can become so absorbed in their subject that they don't notice a whole day has gone by.

Sensory processing differences

Is it sometimes hard to notice or understand how your body feels?

Some neurodivergent people experience differences in their interoception and proprioception, which can help to explain why it can be hard to notice how our bodies feel. Let me explain what I mean:

Interoception

This describes how our brains interpret all of the signals which are being received from internal organs, and it's important because these signals affect our behaviour. For example, if we feel hungry then we eat, if our bladders feel full, we take a toilet break, and if we are too cold, we put on an extra jumper. Interoception differences can also change how we understand or feel pain. If these signals are confused or go unnoticed, you might not realize that you are unwell, thirsty, hungry or sore from sitting hunched over a laptop for hours.

Some students may have also been told they have something called alexithymia. This is thought to be the result of these kinds of differences in interoception.[5] Alexithymia is a term used to describe when people have trouble understanding, recognizing and expressing their own emotions. It can mean that people either 'miss' the bodily clues that tell them about how they are feeling or can become confused about the meanings of these. For example, they might find it hard to differentiate between hunger and tiredness. Alexithymia is considered to be particularly common in autism.[6]

Proprioception

Proprioception describes how our bodies interpret their place in space, so that includes our position and movement. Many neurodivergent students experience challenges here (not just those with dyspraxia), perhaps having balance issues, bumping into things or getting lost.

This can make being in crowded spaces particularly tricky, from the point of view of being able to physically navigate through a space. This can be compounded by differences in the way that many neurodivergent students experience sensory input.

Vestibular system (balance)

The vestibular system is our sense of balance. It is linked very closely to proprioception and the two can influence one another. This doesn't necessarily mean we're falling over, but maybe you stumble a bit more, or you don't feel just right. It could be your sense of balance feeling off.

> *Do you experience differences in processing sensory input?*

If you process sensory input differently, you might find that some of your senses are more 'sensitive' than others. This can involve all eight senses (interoception, proprioception and balance are senses too) and you might find yourself either seeking or avoiding certain kinds of sensory inputs or situations. For example, some find they are very sensitive to noise, lights, textures or tastes and smells. Students often describe how these can sometimes make the world feel overwhelming. For example, busy environments and unfamiliar situations might be challenging. These can also be a source of comfort and pleasure as, if you can identify things which calm your senses, you can use this to your advantage.

The joys and perils of 'bigger picture' thinking

Over the years, I have found that my students are often 'bigger picture' thinkers.

> **Bigger picture thinking** *describes how some people visualize the whole idea, rather than focussing on smaller details. It means they can 'see' the longer-term impacts of their decisions or actions.*

So, if you are a bigger-picture thinker, you probably don't view an issue or problem in simple ways but tend toward thinking about every possible outcome. There are pros and cons to this.

The pros

On one hand, it can result in what we could call 'helpful rumination'. Mulling something over from many different perspectives helps neurodivergent people to be extremely creative in the way they approach anything tricky. It can lead to innovative ideas. When this is combined with detailed specialist knowledge, it can be very valuable, particularly to employers.

The cons

On the other hand, it may also result in feeling overwhelmed or paralysed, as it can seem like there are just too many options to consider. It might also lead to a tendency to catastrophize, which can cause a lot of anxiety. However, it stands to reason that not all of the myriad of possible outcomes to a given situation are positive! So, to me, this seems like a natural response, though I appreciate that it is not always helpful in terms of mental wellbeing and can contribute to feeling overwhelmed and burnt out. The following tip might help.

A tip to stop catastrophizing

When anything feels too much, it's generally good to try and externalize your thoughts and break ideas down into smaller nuggets. You could try writing your thoughts on to sticky notes. Put them up, or throw them away, depending on whether you feel the points are important. You could also try one of the decision-making and problem-solving tools like the Eisenhower matrix in Chapter 3 or Ishikawa diagram in Chapter 4.

Other co-occurring conditions

There are many conditions which can sit alongside neurodivergence. I will mention a few of the most common ones here, but this is by no means an exhaustive list.

Mental health challenges

Many students I work with have been diagnosed with anxiety and/or depression. Research tells us this diagnosis is higher in some parts of the neurodivergent community than in the general population.[7] We often talk this through and we sometimes decide this is unsurprising when they are operating in a world which is dominated by, and designed to suit, neurotypical people. Anecdotally, I have found many later-diagnosed students to have been given a diagnosis of anxiety first. To me, this feels like a natural response to having to manage in environments (often schools) which did not cater for their needs.

Masking can also contribute to mental health challenges,[8] which is something I've described earlier in this chapter.

Rejection-sensitive dysphoria (RSD)

There is increasing evidence that people with ADHD are more likely to experience rejection-sensitive dysphoria.[9] This describes feelings of acute emotional pain in response to perceived failure, rejection or criticism. I have come across this when working with neurodivergence of all kinds. This can make receiving and acting upon feedback feel quite uncomfortable and sometimes threatening. This is tricky because students' work is continually being graded.

Have a look at the section titled 'Using feedback' in Chapter 7, which has a reflective model you can use to make your understanding of feedback feel a bit less personal and more objective.

Pathological demand avoidance

Pathological demand avoidance (PDA) is a feature of some people's neurodivergent profiles, particularly those which include autism.[10] It's a different way of processing when demands, expectations or requests are made of you. If this applies to you, you may instinctively feel a huge amount of pressure when this happens, even if these demands seem to be outwardly 'reasonable' or 'ordinary'.

As a result, you might try to reduce your feelings of anxiety or overwhelm by using strategies like avoidance or refusal. Unfortunately, some students find that other people can misinterpret this response as being negative or even obstructive. This can make it difficult for students to communicate their needs and wants.

 You can try to work out the situations where your demand avoidance is particularly 'front-forward'. Can you see a pattern? Is there anything that you can do to reduce the stressors? Perhaps you can include a period of calm before and after times when you know this might be difficult for you. Can you ask others to make reasonable adjustments to reduce the impact of their demands?

Functional neurological disorder (FND)

This describes difficulties in the way the brain processes and sends information throughout the body. People with FND can have a wide range of variable symptoms which can affect many parts of the body, such as limb weakness (or control) and seizures. Sometimes people with FND can also experience pain and fatigue. There is evidence of some overlap between FND and autism,[11] as well as hypermobility disorders (see below).[12]

Speech, language and communication needs (SLCN)

This term describes a wide range of challenges that an individual might face concerning how they communicate. This can mean a person might struggle to both understand what others are saying and to express themselves in a way that is easy for others to understand. The Royal College of Speech and Language Therapists explains that these needs are some of the most common disabilities in childhood and that there is some evidence of some overlap with some neurodivergent conditions.[13]

Some other physiological conditions

Finally, there are some other co-occurring physical problems which seem more common in neurodivergent students. These can be challenging and painful; for example, issues with gut health or hypermobility (where people have an unusually great range of movement in their joints and sometimes other tissues).[14] There is evidence that the hypermobile type of Ehlers-Danlos syndrome (a connective tissue disorder), in particular, seems to have some overlap with autism.[15]

I know that sometimes students do not show or feel their pain in 'typical' ways, perhaps because of differences in interoception, or because they have not been listened to in the past.

 Medics sometimes don't know about the links between neurodivergence and these conditions. It's okay to tell them!

All of these issues, when combined with a heavy academic workload, can contribute towards overwhelm and, eventually, burnout. However, there are several ways to counter this. Some of the more straightforward ones are listed in the next few paragraphs.

Strategies for preventing and combatting overwhelm

I really want to focus on putting in place long-term strategies to stop you from reaching your limits in the first place, but I thought I would start with a few ideas you can use if you find yourself in a moment of overwhelm.

Quick 'in-the-moment' strategies

* **Grounding yourself** physically and trying to bring your attention back into your body. Try pushing your fingertips together or pushing your palms down on a desk or your back against a wall.

* **Find a quiet place to retreat to.** Place your hands on your abdomen and focus on breathing in and out slowly from your belly (feel it moving in and out).

* **Focus just on 'now and next'.** Now is literally what you are doing now, right that second. For example, 'Now I will breathe deeply from my abdomen to help calm myself.' Next is what you will do immediately after, for example, 'Next I will slowly walk to the library.'

* **Use items in your 'rescue box'** to help yourself feel better.

How to make a 'rescue box'

This is a box where you can keep things that you find comforting. Keep it nearby so that if you are feeling overwhelmed you have something ready to open to help you feel better. Make your box on a day when you are feeling good. If you like, you can use a small bag instead (something like a drawstring shoe bag works well); that way you can take it with you.

Contents might include:

- something which smells nice – an essential oil, some herbs, lip balm, perfume or aftershave

- something that feels nice – choose a texture that you enjoy – this could be stretchy, crunchy, smooth, rough or soft

- a photograph of something you like to look at – that could be related to an interest, a beautiful scene, your pet, friends or family

- an enjoyable snack – make sure this is something that doesn't go bad quickly

- a tea bag or sachet of hot chocolate – something to remind yourself to have a drink
- some motivational quotes or affirmations, but only if you like these – some people, including myself, find them super-irritating!

Now, let's look at some longer-term strategies you can put in place to help support sustainable study practices moving forward.

Pacing strategies

The first and most important idea here is that of pacing. Many of you will recognize a pattern of boom and bust. For example, some students tell me that they can revise all night for an exam the next day but then have a mental and physical 'crash' immediately after. Some can recover quickly after this, but this becomes harder when intense periods of stress are more sustained, like during exam periods.

Pacing is a way of balancing your activity levels (both mental and physical) with your need to rest and recuperate to avoid this kind of negative cycle. We'll look at the three strategies listed below in more detail:

* energy accounting
* energy reduction
* planning ahead.

Energy accounting

With this idea, you need to think about things which give you energy and things which deplete it. You can list these in two columns as part of your daily to-do list. This helps you to understand why you are particularly exhausted some days and how to avoid this happening.

There is a range of ways to envisage this. Some like to think of themselves as being a bit like a rechargeable battery; others think about there being an accounting ledger with debits and credits.

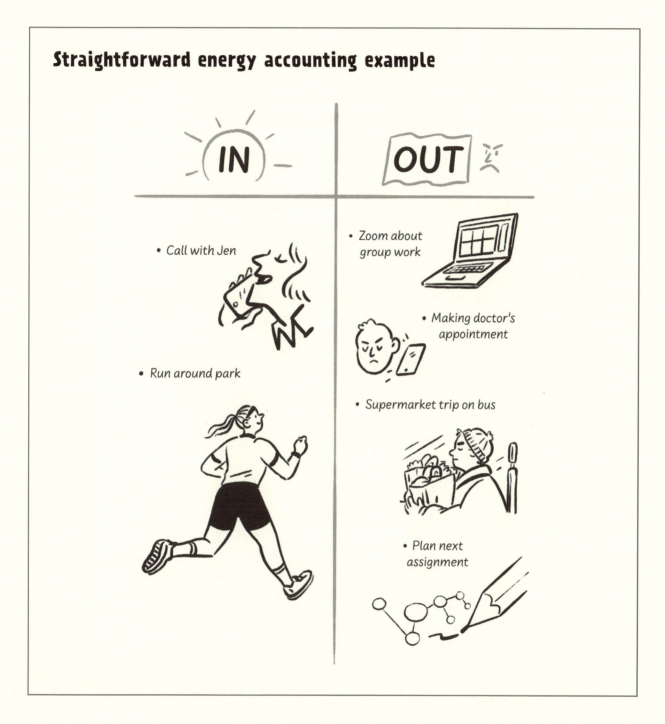

Straightforward energy accounting example

IN
- Call with Jen
- Run around park

OUT
- Zoom about group work
- Making doctor's appointment
- Supermarket trip on bus
- Plan next assignment

Here you can see this student's list is unbalanced as there are more items written in the 'out' column. That means on that particular day they are likely to feel quite tired and stressed. They can take steps to adjust the balance by moving or redistributing things in the 'out' column. Alternatively, they might add items to the 'in' column which will help them to feel revitalized, such as doing an activity they find soothing. For example, one student I worked with found baking relaxing so would make bread if they needed to regain some energy.

Some students find this a little simplistic, as the items on their 'energy out' list are not equally weighted. So, they could consider giving a weighting to each activity to help them see more easily if their energy levels are well balanced.

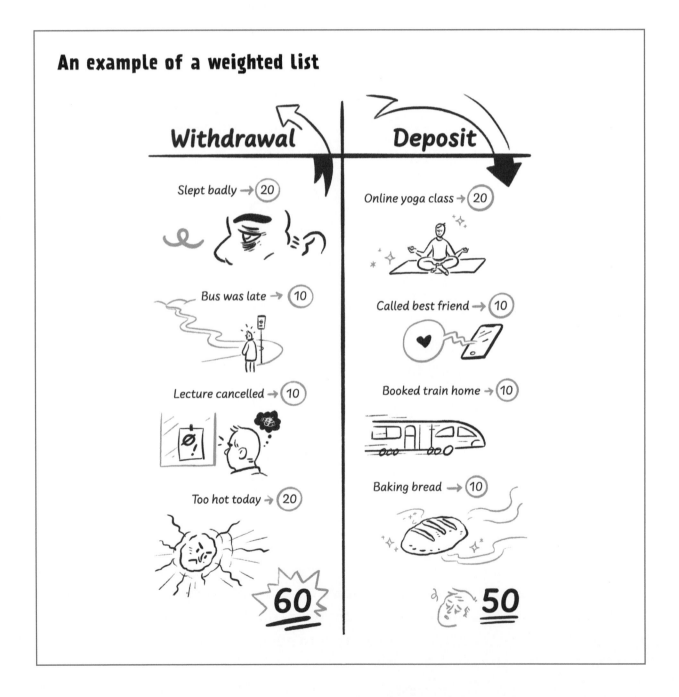

You can use this daily 'diary' to record your energy levels (to help with pacing).

Daily diary record

Withdrawal	Cost	Deposit	Benefit
Example: shopping trip	*10*	*Example: jog around the park*	*15*
Total		Total	

Energy reduction

Alternatively, you might just think about yourself as having a finite amount of energy for a given day and use any method you like to represent this.

 One well-known strategy is the spoon theory, which was an idea developed by Christine Miserandino.[16] Originally intended for people with chronic ill-health, it has also been adopted by many in the neurodivergent community. This is how it works:

* Energy is represented by spoons.

* Each activity or interaction uses several spoons, the number of which depends upon the individual 'cost' to you. For example, a shower might take away one spoon, but a dental appointment will remove five.

* Your aim is not to run out of spoons.

* You can decide how many spoons you start the day with, but a round number like ten can be a good starting place.

However, I have found that many students find the connection between spoons and energy a bit tenuous! If that applies to you, then you can use a different analogy.

> **Example of an alternative energy accounting method: bean counting**
>
> This is the idea of starting the day with some imaginary beans. It helps that we sometimes say to a person with lots of energy, 'You're full of beans today!' Choose the number of beans you start with – ten can be a good number. Take away the beans as the day progresses.
>
> If this is still too abstract (and perhaps if you like to have something tactile to fiddle with) you can have ten physical things which you transfer from one pocket to another. That way you can physically feel when your energy is depleting. Choose something small and light! Ten small coins can work well, as can buttons.

Planning ahead if boom and bust are unavoidable

I want to help you avoid a self-defeating cycle of boom and bust, but this is not always realistic. For example, you may have three days of intense exams and we can't do very much to avoid you feeling exhausted by this, even if you have sensible reasonable adjustments in place such as regular breaks and extra time.

In this situation, it's important to remember that you will need time to rest and recover. So, try to plan a few days of downtime after this stressful period.

 *Write a to-do list for the days **after** the exams **before** they happen. You will almost certainly be too worn out to think of where to start afterwards! Ensure that your list is gentle to begin with and that you have scheduled regular breaks for yourself.*

The next strategy can help you work out if any of your sensory processing differences can help boost your energy too.

Playing to your personal sensory profile

While sensory processing differences can sometimes be a barrier to learning (such as sensitivity to sound), these can also be used to your advantage.

Therapists sometimes use the idea of a 'sensory diet' when designing programmes to support people with sensory processing challenges. These aim to prevent sensory and emotional overload by meeting a person's sensory needs.

You can think about this idea for yourself. Everyone will be very different with this, but it is worth thinking about whether there is anything you can proactively do to support your sensory preferences. You could start by asking yourself these three questions:

> *Do I find any particular textures calming or comforting?*

> *Do I find any particular sights or sounds soothing?*

> *Do I find the sensation of pressure relaxing?*

If you can answer 'yes' to any of these questions, you can find ways to incorporate sensory preferences into your study routine. This can be particularly helpful during exams and revision periods when you may well need to pay more attention to your mental wellbeing.

Here are some of the things you can consider.

Textures

In my experience, many students have preferences for different kinds of textures. For example, some students like furry or soft textures, and if so, a blanket or cushion on their lap can feel soothing. Other students like the feel of velvet or silk, and I've known some to wear scarves made of these fabrics.

Generally, it can be quite useful to have something to fiddle with as a form of distraction. If you can combine this with your sensory likes, then this is a win-win situation.

You can take physical objects that you find soothing to lectures or school. You might need to check with your school first as I have found that some can be very peculiar about this. If you are encountering resistance, think about choosing something unobtrusive such as a small ball of sticky-tac to silently play with, which can be quite satisfying.

> ### Making a sensory box or tray
>
> You can keep a selection of small items which you find to be sensorily satisfying close to you while you study. Keep these on a small tray (can be noisy) or in a lid from a small box (quieter but not so pretty). For example, a student who likes smooth, cold, spherical objects keeps a few pebbles and marbles on theirs. These are useful to fiddle with quietly during stressful meetings or online lectures.

Sights or sounds

If you enjoy particular sounds, try to find a way to incorporate these into your study routine. For example, you might play the sounds of the rainforest or breaking waves while you study. This can also be useful to signal a change of activity, so always playing the same music for the same type of 'event' can help to get your brain into the appropriate 'mode'. For example, I always mark my students' work to music by the same artist.

In terms of sights that you find soothing, there is a balance to be struck between something you find too interesting and something you find calming. One student (in shared accommodation) hated the geometric wallpaper in their room as it gave them visual stress and was truly ugly. They stuck a large square of fake grass on the wall behind their workspace which was more visually soothing but not too distracting.

Physical pressure

The final question around pressure is more complicated but something that I have found many students enjoy. We have to be careful here because if you are a young person there can be implications for growth. This means I would caution against using the weighted lap-mats etc. that you can buy online unless you have received professional advice first. A clinician can tell you what weight is safe for your build.

That said, there are some things that you can do to help give yourself that satisfactory feeling of pressure. Simply pausing and standing up to push your back or your arms against a wall can give you a nice sensory break. You could also try jumping up and down on the spot or doing some wall-press-ups for a similar sensation.

You can combine your sensory preferences with the pacing ideas above.

Case study example: combining pacing and sensory preferences

Ameena is using the idea of having a finite amount of energy each day and so imagines that she starts the day with ten beans.

She has to attend a university in central London three days a week. She must travel by tube, which is hot, packed and extremely noisy. She wears noise-cancelling headphones and fiddles with a smooth stone in her pocket to distract her. It is still a sensory nightmare and causes significant anxiety.

> The journey to university takes away five of her beans before she even starts to learn. She urgently needs to regain some energy, otherwise she will run out of beans before she must make her return journey. If she doesn't, she knows from experience that it will lead to her feeling awful and being 'shutdown' for the next few days while her brain and body try to recover.
>
> Ameena knows that she finds being in natural environments calming. She likes to hear birdsong and to feel the wind on her skin. She plans a detour so that her walk from the tube station to campus takes her through a park. This takes longer but gives her some time to breathe and resettle herself. She has regained three beans.
>
> In fact, Ameena often uses nature and natural sounds as a form of self-soothing. She plays the sounds of the ocean in the background when she is revising and watches natural world documentaries before she goes to bed.

Finding the joy

Studying is tough and can be stressful. I often say to my students, 'Where's the joy?' when they present me with a long, relentless study plan. It is important to keep note of the things that make you feel joyful, those light spots in your life. Please be kind to yourself!

Here are a few ideas:

* Try making a list of 'joyful things' and putting it somewhere you can see, so that if you are starting to feel stressed or overwhelmed, you could try doing something from your list. For example, a student might love to cycle, so if they have lots of revision, they make sure they go for a ride at lunchtime to break up the day. This helps them to feel mentally and physically refreshed.

* Try to build in a series of small rewards for yourself. These can be simple things like treating yourself to a nice drink, watching a favourite film or playing a video game.

* Keep a daily journal or note of positive things. Some of my students jot these down in their phones before they go to sleep as it helps them end the day on a happy note. These don't have to be 'big' things. For example, you might have particularly enjoyed a takeaway coffee or listened to a new song by your favourite artist. If you are feeling a bit low, it can be helpful to look back through your notes to remind yourself that there have been bright spots in your week.

You can use this table to write your joyful things list.

Things that bring me joy	✓	✓	✓	✓
Example: walking the dog	✗			

Staying connected

Staying connected with others is also useful but not always easy for neurodivergent students. Many educational institutions have clubs or societies for students with declared 'conditions'. You can think about joining one of these, as there is often comfort to be found with like-minded people who truly 'get it'.

If that's not for you, then you could consider joining other groups which might be related to your interests, whether they be subject related, sports orientated or something completely different.

It is also easy to lose touch with friends when you are so busy with your studies. Try to check in with friends regularly.

> *Students sometimes worry that their friends will want to meet up and they won't have time. It's okay to message, 'Hey, I'm thinking of you. How are you? I am so busy with college right now, but didn't want to lose touch.'*

Food, exercise and sleep

I am not an expert in these areas; however, they definitely need some thought. Common sense, as well as research, tells us these are important. I will include some simple self-help strategies here, but if any of these areas are becoming an issue for you (that means they are interfering with your daily life and functioning), I would urge you to contact a professional for further support and advice.

Sleep

Sleep can be a particularly thorny problem and we know that this is true for many neurodivergent individuals, with difficulties being particularly well documented in ADHD.[17] Sleep studies tell us that sleeping poorly can cut learning ability by up to 40 per cent and, equally, sleeping well after a period of learning can help to embed new information into our memory systems.[18]

If sleep is difficult for you, you might try the following:

* Go to bed and get up at the same time each day so that your body gets into a routine.
* Make your bedroom a comfortable environment. Try to avoid too much stimulation in the room. This is hard if your work desk is also there. If this applies, try to keep your desk out of your immediate eye line when lying down, and turn over any work so that it isn't shouting 'deadlines!' at you from the corner! You could lay a pillowcase on top of your desk at night to cover it all up.
* Use an eye mask and/or earplugs to reduce sensory input.
* Create a mini routine around bedtime. For example, make a warm drink, put on comfy pyjamas, play some soft music or read a book. You could also

incorporate elements which play to your sensory profile, such as stroking a furry blanket if that's something you find soothing. The repetition of this routine is important as it can help 'trick' your body and mind into recognizing that now it is time for sleep, each time you complete it. It might take a while for this to work, but keep going!

* If you find gentle pressure soothing, try tucking yourself in tightly, or experiment with heavy blankets.

* Avoid reading messages, scrolling through social media or playing on other electronic devices while you are in bed. Turn your phone on to 'do not disturb' at nighttime. This is because you are trying to calm your mind, not stimulate it.

* If you wake up at night, do not be tempted to pick up your phone. Use your self-soothing routine again; perhaps play some soft music or read for a little while.

Food

There is evidence that consuming a wide variety of nutritious food can help attention, learning and mood.[19] However, my experience is that the majority of students find maintaining a decent diet very tricky, particularly if they are living away from home. There is a great deal of organization required to source and prepare healthy meals, which can feel overwhelming. Sensory sensitivities around food can also be a challenge.

Here are some strategies which have worked for students I have supported:

* Build a trip to the supermarket into a routine, i.e. go to the shops every Monday evening and shop for that week.

* Create a list of quick, nutritious meals on your phone. The internet can be a very good source of information for these.

* Use AI to help you to create meal plans. This is quite fun to play around with. You could try putting a list of items from your cupboard and fridge into the chat prompt and ask it to find recipes. Alternatively, you can ask it to find recipes for a given budget. Try typing in something like: 'I have a budget of £40. I need to

make seven meals. Find me seven recipes.' It can also create shopping lists for you and help you incorporate any dietary requirements or sensory preferences.

* Keep some healthy snacks in your cupboard so that you have something nutritious to reach for on days when you can't face meal preparation. Allergies permitting, things like nuts and milk-based drinks can work well for this.

* If you live in shared accommodation, you can coordinate with other students so that you are each responsible for a meal on a given night every week. This can feel like a lot of responsibility, but it does mean that you only have to think about one meal per week. This works best for students without any food-related sensitivities.

Exercise

There is evidence that aerobic exercise can improve focus[20] immediately before a study session and that even moderate activity (like walking) can help with information recall.[21] Exercise has also been shown to improve mood, particularly for those who have lower mood to begin with.[22]

To help motivate yourself to exercise regularly you could try the following

- Build some regular time into your schedule for exercise. This could be as straightforward as walking to college twice a week, rather than getting the bus.

- Join a club or society. Most schools, colleges and universities have a range of different sports and activities which you can try. Look for something that you enjoy; it should not be a trial! For example, if you like dancing there will probably be a dance society. You might prefer something a little less frenetic. I have worked with several students who dislike the physical sensation of feeling sweaty, which makes exercise tricky. They might try something like Tai Chi or yoga which are still physically demanding but slower paced.

- Exercise at home. Some students detest the idea of group exercise. There is a huge range of online resources that you can use. Be careful to go slowly and gently with this and ask a clinician for advice if you are at risk of injury or have other underlying health issues. Often, they can recommend safer online resources. For example, the NHS in the UK has a set of openly available 'fitness studio exercise' videos.

 You could try incorporating water into your exercise routine. If you live near a body of water (the sea, a lake or a river) you could try walking nearby as there is evidence that this is psychologically soothing.[23] Studies also show that swimming has beneficial cognitive effects.[24]

Do we speak the same language? A note about Double Empathy Theory

When I am talking to my neurodivergent students, I often explain difficulties in communication as being a bit like trying to understand a foreign language. Neurotypical people don't always understand neurodivergent people, and vice versa. It's no one's fault, it's just a different way of communicating. With some willingness to try, and understanding from both parties, it's usually possible to reach a good level of understanding.

In autism research, this could be seen as one element of the 'double empathy problem'.[25]

__Double Empathy Theory__ describes challenges people with different life experiences can have interacting and empathizing with each other. It stresses the need for mutual respect and understanding. It does not make any problems with communication the 'fault' of the autistic person because communication is a two-way process.

> This could also explain why students often enjoy belonging to societies and groups which comprise other neurodivergent folk. It's comfortable and easier to be around people who communicate in the same way.
>
> Something that you could consider to help open those channels of communication is to be open about your neurodivergence. However, this is not a straightforward topic so I have given you some ideas to think about in the next section as looking after yourself and your needs is important for long-term self-care.

Self-advocacy strategies

You are likely to have to advocate for yourself, both while you are studying and in the wider world. While knowledge and understanding of neurodivergence are increasing, there's still a long way to go. I'm guessing that many of you will have already come across professionals who do not adjust their approach to meet your needs. So, while it would be understandable for you to shout at me: 'It's not my job to educate other people about my neurodivergence', it can be very helpful to start developing your self-advocacy skills. This is something that will stand you in good stead for the future, particularly in the workplace.

If your educational institution knows that you are neurodivergent, you will probably have some kind of inclusion plan. The name of this will be different depending on where you are studying, but it will most likely include details about:

* your particular blend of neurodivergence and how this affects your learning; for example, dyslexia may impact reading speeds

* steps that can be taken to support you with this; for example, provide extra time for reading and give reading material before lectures

* the reasonable adjustments (accommodations) you are entitled to; for example, extra time in assessments and examinations.

Most schools, colleges and universities will distribute this information to your teachers and tutors. Some are fantastic and will ensure they are providing you with the right kind of support. However, in my experience, others will neither read nor act upon this information. That means it is a good idea to take proactive steps to ensure that everyone **fully** understands your needs. If you are still at school, a parent or carer can do this on your behalf. Here is an example of an email which could be sent to a lecturer:

Dear Margie,

I am looking forward to attending your lectures. I wanted to let you know a little bit more about me so that we can work together to ensure that I achieve to the very best of my abilities.

I have a diagnosis of autism and ADHD, which can affect my studies in the following ways:

- I can find it hard to concentrate in lectures and might need more time to process information. Having notes in advance really helps with this.

- I may need short breaks to be able to refocus.

- I may need to check my understanding often, so I will ask lots of questions.

- I will need extra time for in-class assessments as well as for exams and assignments.

My autism and ADHD also mean that I am well read and enthusiastic about my subject, and I am very much looking forward to studying this year.

Please let me know if you would like to discuss any of the above.

Thank you,

Arwen

> *Do this first, right at the start of the term. Do not wait to see if anyone contacts you to ask what your needs are. Be proactive!*

Sometimes students tell me they feel they are being 'too pushy' when they do this, but there are some real benefits:

* Support can be put into action from day one.

* It helps to build a good relationship with those who are teaching you as it opens a dialogue.

* You can re-send the same email at the start of each new academic year, or every time you encounter new staff.

* If things don't go according to plan (I hope they do), you have some paperwork to refer back to and say 'I told you so!'

A note about reasonable adjustments

Depending on where you live, there will be laws and regulations in place which entitle you to various 'reasonable adjustments' (or accommodations) based on your needs. In the UK, these mainly fall under the terms of the Equality Act 2010.[26] These oblige educational institutions to be flexible to accommodate students who meet the law's definition of being 'disabled' so that they are not disadvantaged compared to their non-disabled peers. It is worth taking some time to read up on what legislation says about your rights in terms of education. This will help you to get a clearer idea of what additional support may be available to you. This applies to all levels of education. In terms of higher education, at the time of writing, the system of support for UK students (Disabled Students Allowance) is under review, so it isn't sensible for me to talk about this here.

However, something that will doubtless remain the case is that educational institutions will always have a dedicated individual or team responsible for 'looking after' students who have any kind of so-called additional needs. It is worth getting to know who these people are within your own context so that you know where to go for help and advice. At the university level, student unions are also often excellent sources of information.

Disclosure

Of course, all of the self-advocacy advice given above relies on the fact that you have disclosed your neurodivergence to your tutors/teacher and probably to your peers. However, I know from discussions with students that this is often a complex area to consider, particularly for those who have been late-diagnosed.

This is a very individual decision and, despite changing attitudes, there remains stigma in some settings, which can make disclosure uncomfortable. You are the best judge of your environment and will know whether you feel safe (or want) to do so.

If you are finding the idea of disclosing difficult, you could ask yourself a question: Do I see my neurodivergence as being some kind of deficiency rather than as being a different way of thinking?

If you do find yourself feeling like you are not quite 'enough' in some way, this may have been encouraged by the fact that most diagnostic assessments are based upon what a person 'can't do' compared to their neurotypical contemporaries. In fact, lots of our systems (including things like schools) are based on a model that looks to fix things that are perceived as being 'wrong', rather than embracing the full range of neurodiversity.

You could think about whether you may have unintentionally absorbed some of this negative messaging around your own neurodivergence. I promise I'm not blaming you if you have! It's impossible to separate our actions, feelings and sense of self-identity from the social world in which we live.[27] I just gently suggest that it's something you might like to ponder.

If this **is** something you would like to think about, and you would like to rebalance any negative self-thoughts, you could try one of these ideas:

* Write a big, bold list of all of the skills you have. Think about things like problem-solving, being detail conscious, seeing patterns in things, verbal skills, being creative etc. You can keep your list on your phone so that it's always with you, or pin it up on the wall near your workspace. If you have trouble working out what to include, you can look back over past feedback and note the positive comments, or (if you are feeling brave) ask trusted people close to you what your best skills are.

* Keep a running list of your achievements. Write down that good assignment score, that exam you passed or the presentation that went well. You can include personal successes here too. Maybe you have joined a new society or been to an event that you found challenging. Remember to congratulate yourself.

* Think about your personal values. You could write these down too. Focussing on these can help to remove some of the external 'noise', which can be negative. For example, being honest and straightforward might be a core value. If you know that you are living your life in a way that aligns with this value, that can feel reassuring.

Signs that things might be going wrong

It can be useful to recognize the signs when things might be going wrong for you. The main thing to think about here is whether you are **feeling and behaving differently from what is normal for you**. If you're not sure, try asking someone else who is close to you if they have noticed differences.

For example, you might:

* experience more difficulties with sleep than usual
* have changes in your appetite
* have lost motivation to go to classes and complete assignments
* feel that you are not good enough to achieve in your work
* have more trouble focussing on things/completing tasks than is usual for you
* withdraw from those around you
* not be taking care of your appearance or hygiene.

Please talk to someone as **soon as you can** if you feel you are feeling overwhelmed and perhaps are heading towards burnout. Schools, colleges and universities have pastoral teams who can help you. If you find talking difficult, you can always email. Some organizations will have text messaging systems that you can use which many students prefer. If it is too overwhelming to do that yourself, tell someone else that you trust and ask them to help you access services on your behalf. The important thing to do is to reach out for help, quickly, so that support can be put in place.

Please remember that you are not 'a bother' if you ask for help. Staff within education are paid to support you and, in my experience, they do their job because they genuinely want to help students.

We've focused on the things that can be tricky in this chapter, so now it's time to move on to look at the study skills strategies that can help you reduce any feelings of being overwhelmed. The next chapter looks at how being (and feeling) more organized can support sustainable study practices.

Let's recap

In this chapter we have covered:

- definitions of overwhelm and burnout
- some common experiences (hyper-focus, experiences of time, understanding how bodies feel)
- bigger picture thinking
- co-occurring conditions
- pacing strategies (energy accounting)
- planning to avoid boom and bust
- playing to your sensory profile
- finding the joy
- staying connected
- food, exercise, sleep
- self-advocacy
- disclosure
- signs that things might be going wrong.

 Key takeaway points from this chapter

- Your mental and physical wellbeing always comes first.
- Pacing can really help to manage the stress that comes with studying.
- Make sure you are getting reasonable adjustments you are entitled to and are using all of the available support.
- Ask for help if you need it – there are people whose job it is to support you, so use them!

Chapter 3

GETTING ORGANIZED

Introduction

Having good personal organization can **really** help to reduce study-related stress. We can think of this as being like the foundation level of a house. Shoddy foundations may last for a while, but eventually, the building will begin to crumble, whereas a solid foundation gives a firm base on which to build.

The same applies when you are studying. On the surface, you may be getting along fine with less-than-ideal study habits, such as working through the night to hit deadlines. However, things can go wrong quite quickly when there is increased pressure or an unexpected event. Often this happens when there are competing deadlines, exams or illness. Having good personal organization systems already in place can help you manage these stressful times much more easily.

There are three main components to getting organized that we'll consider in this chapter:

1. organizing your space

2. organizing your time

3. organizing your materials.

How to organize your space

The first thing to do is to make a calm, designated study space. However, this isn't always easy when homes can be crowded and busy. Few of us are lucky enough to have our own study or office. However, it is a good idea to have somewhere where you can keep your materials and have everything you need immediately at hand. There are some important things to consider when establishing your space.

Avoid distraction

First, think carefully about the levels of potential distraction around your chosen spot, particularly if you have ADHD within your profile. A kitchen table in a busy house may be large and comfortable, but the potential for random chatting is extremely high!

Find a suitable space

Generally, it's best to find a quiet space where unsolicited auditory and visual distractions are kept to an absolute minimum. However, the word 'unsolicited' in this sentence is doing an awful lot of work. This is because for some students a level of background noise, which they can manage, is helpful and is actually less disturbing than complete silence. This doesn't have to be music. For some, gentle repeatedly rhythmic sounds, such as waves, waterfalls or other white noise, are very helpful. This might take some experimentation.

Sometimes we can't avoid working in a noisy environment, so students often wear headphones, particularly those with autism in their profile. There are also several in-ear noise reduction products on the market, which many students say work well for them.

If you are thinking about getting noise-cancelling headphones, I suggest borrowing some first to try out. Several autistic students have told me they can feel 'suffocating', and have regretted spending so much money. Some in-ear noise reduction products have longer return policies so you can try out the product and get a refund if you don't like them.

Visual distraction can be just as difficult as unwanted sound, particularly if you have visual stress, which is fairly common in neurodivergent profiles, especially those which include dyslexia. That means it is important to think about lighting; for example, positioning yourself where bright light shines neither directly in your eyes nor on your screen.

Equally, having uninteresting walls around you is far less distracting than having a pinboard covered in photos directly in your sight line. If you are likely to be distracted by what you can see from a window, then you could use some kind of opaque covering or blind to block your view.

Do not disturb

It's also important to ensure that other people understand that you need a protected space to study in. You could discuss this with other members of your household. Some students have made (polite) signs for the back of their chairs or doors, reminding their housemates not to disturb them while they are studying.

Here's a 'do not disturb' sign that you could print and use!

Once you have found your space, make sure that you have the basics in place so that you can begin to study as soon as you sit down. That means having writing materials to hand and perhaps a pack of sticky notes. Many students also keep a large water bottle at their workstation to remind themselves to drink (particularly if they are taking medication which can lead to a dry mouth, like some ADHD meds).

A final comment about phones: many like to charge these via USB on their laptops. Please think carefully about how likely you are to be distracted by your phone while you are studying. If you know that you are someone who cannot ignore a notification, it's best to charge it somewhere where it is not in your sight line.

This probably all sounds a bit dull, but I wouldn't expect you to study unrelentingly in this space, which is where managing your time comes into the equation.

How to organize your time

 Just to repeat my introductory advice: remember to try a range of strategies until you find one that works for you, as different profiles and different students will have different needs!

Those who are autistic and have ADHD (sometimes known as AuDHD) can find this area particularly challenging and might need to experiment more than others. It seems to me that sometimes students crave chaos but thrive on routine, which can be a very tricky balance to negotiate.

Rhythm and routine

Remember when I mentioned the common tendency towards hyper-focus and/or monotropism in Chapter 2? We know there are advantages and disadvantages here, but what we must do is avoid some of the pitfalls which can lead to students forgetting to attend to their basic needs. Establishing a routine can help to avoid these. Therefore, whatever your particular blend of neurodivergence, it is a good idea to find a regular rhythm of studying which works for you.

Here are some things to bear in mind when you are deciding on a routine that feels right:

* Think about the time of day. When are you most alert? Some students find they work best in the afternoon, while others find they slump after lunch. Plan your most difficult things to do when your brain is usually the most awake. If you are on medication which affects your level of focus, you should factor this in too.

* You are not a machine! You need some time off from studying. Remember to build in plenty of breaks and ideally one day a week when you will not study at all.

* Remember to move. This is good for body and mind. There is some research which demonstrates a correlation between levels of physical activity and

academic achievement.[1,2] When you take a break, make sure that you physically get up and away from your computer.

 Some students have almost ridiculous levels of content to get through (yes, I'm looking at you, law and medical students). That means they often can't 'afford' a whole day off a week. It is still vital to build in some self-care and some study breaks, perhaps to exercise, have a quick coffee with a friend or just take in some air.

Organizing your time: using the idea of layers

The majority of my students like to use a kind of 'tiered' or layered time planning system. First, they create a big picture, overall plan for the whole academic year so they can see at a glance the key deadlines and holidays. Then, throughout the year, they create smaller study plans for themselves which break tasks down into manageable chunks. The final step is to ensure they keep daily lists of tasks to be completed. You could think of this as being a little like a pyramid:

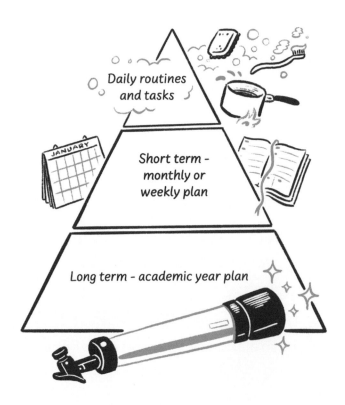

There are many different ways of practically putting these plans into place. Some like to use digital time planning tools, such as Google Calendar or Microsoft Outlook. There are also paid-for digital planning apps. Others prefer to use a paper diary or wall planner. Many use a combination of both!

The advice given below is intended for general use during term time. You might like to tweak things a little if you are revising for exams (this is covered in more depth in Chapter 8 'Achieving Your Goals in Exams').

Long term – academic yearly planning

Often neurodivergent students are excellent at looking at the bigger picture and seeing how wider concerns are related. This creates the foundation for your time planning.

Create a visual overview of your whole course

You might like to play to this 'bigger picture' strength by creating a visual representation of your course so that you can see at a glance how it all fits together.

This example is from a student starting a computer science degree. The student has shown their course progression as a kind of cycle (just using a standard word processing graphic template). They have added their assessment deadlines around the edges of this cycle.

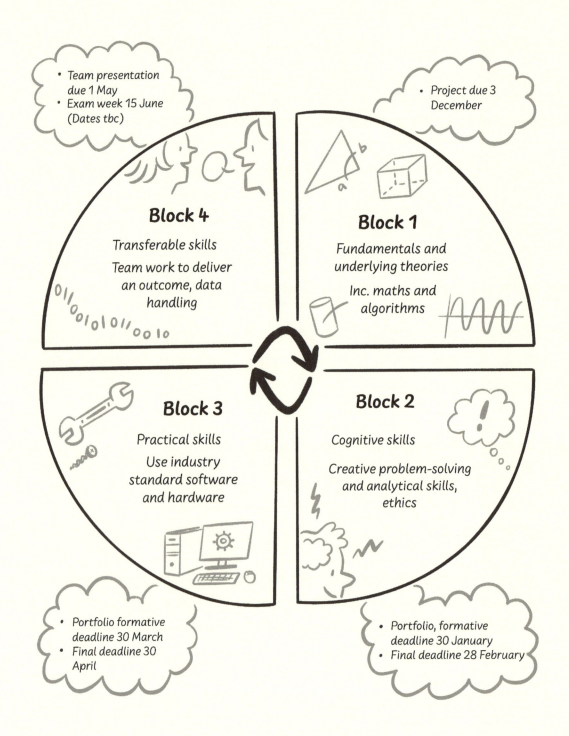

There are other ways you could try representing your course overview too. For example, you could create a flowchart or mind map.

Make a yearly plan

Once you have a good 'feel' for how your studies are related, it can help to be able to view the whole academic year at a glance. In particular, making a yearly plan makes the grouping of simultaneous deadlines visually obvious. If you can see this in advance, you can work out how best to manage the stress of competing priorities.

However, I am not a huge fan of using digital-only planners when it comes to getting this kind of yearly overview. That's because screen size can limit bigger picture thinking ability as you can usually only view limited periods. This is where an old-fashioned, large-scale paper wall planner comes into its own. This doesn't stop you from putting deadline reminders etc. into a digital diary too. Wall planners are a useful additional tool, not a replacement for digital systems.

If you would like to try using a wall planner, I would suggest:

* buying the biggest academic wall planner you can find

* using colour coding (they usually come with coloured sticky dots) – creating your own colour key for different subjects and activities

* putting all of the key deadlines on to your planner – doing this in the first week of your course

* adding in the holidays too and any trips or activities you have booked – it's nice to have something to look forward to

* sticking it up in your sight line, by your workspace (unless that is too stressful, then keep it nearby).

Short term – weekly or monthly planning

You might also need to create smaller plans so that you can break tasks down. For example, you could have two assignments due in the same week. You can see from your large wall planner that this is happening (because the coloured sticky dots are all gathered in a group), but it doesn't really tell you how to manage that. This is where a more detailed shorter-term plan can work well.

Here is an example of an assignment-planning document which covers just over a month:

Assignment	Due date	Task planning	Undertake tasks between
Global societies	17 May	Review source materials	12 April to 15 April
		Planning	16 April to 19 April
		Drafting	20 April to 26 April
		Finalizing	27 April and 1 May
International relations	19 May	Review source materials	2 to 5 May
		Planning	6 to 7 May
		Drafting	8 to 14 May
		Finalizing	15 to 18 May

Can you see that deadlines for this student's assignments almost coincide? Please note that I **would not** advise trying to write both assignments simultaneously. Doing this can be very confusing and will not play to the real strengths that many students have in terms of being able to focus on a topic. It also means that you might miss important themes, arguments or ideas. **Do one at a time wherever you can**. Many neurodivergent students will have accommodations (reasonable adjustments) made for them in terms of deadlines. If you are entitled to a deadline extension because of your neurodivergence, you can use this to help manage competing deadlines.

 Here's a blank monthly table for you to use if you'd like to.

Assignment	Due date	Task planning	Undertake tasks between
Example: Introduction to culture	24 March	Review lectures	1 to 3 March
		Select source material	4 to 6 March
		Plan	7 to 12 March
		Draft	13 to 20 March
		Finalize	20 to 22 March

Daily routines and tasks

It's also very useful to break your time down into smaller chunks so that you have some method of working out what you need to do on a day-to-day basis.

You won't be surprised to know that I am going to start by saying there are many different ways to do this. It **is** important to have some kind of structure, and I have provided some ideas below.

Using the structure of a school day

Sometimes periods of transition can pose a particular challenge to your personal organization skills. When we are in high school, routines and rhythms are imposed on us by the system. We have set times to break, to eat and to learn. However, when we are sent on study leave at the end of high school, or we arrive at college or university, this structure is largely removed. The fact that some courses now provide a blend of online learning and face-to-face lectures has blurred the boundaries between study and home even further.

If you can relate to this scenario and you feel comfortable with the rhythm of the school day, you can think about imposing the same structure upon yourself on the days when you are not physically attending classes. This has several benefits, not least the fact that breaks are in-built, which avoids the risk of forgetting to eat or drink. Several of my college and university students have effectively used this technique. However, I do like to remind them that at high school, students usually move between rooms regularly throughout the day! That movement is an important factor in being able to refocus. You can build this into your routine by ensuring that at the end of each study period, you physically leave your workspace, for example, to get a drink or briefly stretch your legs outside.

However, some students will find this kind of rigid routine far too constraining. That's tricky to manage if you are still in high school as you have little power to influence the structure of your day. However, there are some techniques you can use to help you try and maintain your focus, whatever your educational stage or age, which are described in Chapter 5 'Managing in Class and Note-taking in Lectures'.

Using anchor points

If having a rigid daily structure fills you with dread, then you could try using the idea of having some anchor points in your days instead. An anchor point is something that you do at the same time, on the same day each week. In this way, you can impose some structure upon yourself to scaffold your days, without necessarily dictating each element of this. This still gives you a framework but with more freedom to decide what you will study and when. Using anchor points can be particularly helpful when lectures and classes are finished and you have gone on to study or revision leave.

The first thing to consider here is the structure of your week. During term time, most students will have a repeating pattern to work with. This pattern tends to be more regular for high school students than it is for college or university students. Your aim here is to create a similar repeating pattern of anchor points. To determine your own anchor points, think carefully about your days and the mini-routines you may have already established.

Anchor points: an example

Marianne has a fairly standard morning routine. She gets up, has a cup of coffee, takes a shower and eats a quick breakfast. This rarely changes, so she makes this her first anchor point.

Her second anchor point is at lunchtime because she always tries to eat around noon.

She decides to have a regular coffee break at 3pm, so makes this her third anchor point.

Her final anchor point for the day is her bedtime routine, which is always pretty much the same. She cleanses her face, cleans her teeth, pops on her pyjamas and then reads in bed for about half an hour.

 It is important that the timing of anchor points is regular, otherwise there will be no structure at all!

Using study windows

As an alternative, even more flexible way of working, you can use the idea of study windows. Some people call this 'time-blocking', but I think that phrasing this as a window of opportunity feels more positive.

This is where you look at your weekly timetable and work out the opportunities you will have to study. These become repeating windows of opportunity to study. You can highlight these times physically on your wall planner or digitally on your phone calendar. It's up to you to decide what you study during each study window, but this should be a regular study routine.

 Often students find that putting a study window straight after an anchor point works well for them.

Here is an example of a day using anchor points and study windows on the weekdays that a student is not attending college:

Monday and Wednesday daily routine	
Morning anchor point	Breakfast at 9am Create daily to-do list
Study window	9.30am to 12.30pm Formal break: 15 mins at 10.45 am Remember to move!
Lunch anchor point	Lunch at 1pm Review daily to-do list
Study window	2pm to 5pm Formal break: 15 mins at 3.15pm Remember to move!
End of study day anchor point	5pm Warm drink Final review of to-do list Turn off computer

Note that I have written 'formal break' here. These are when you will always break. However, you are almost certain to need to have smaller breaks in your studying if you are to keep focused – at least once every hour. That is fine. Set a timer for five minutes, walk away, and then come back and re-settle.

Using daily task lists

Lists are underrated! These can be complex or as straightforward as you need them to be, either handwritten or digital. Whatever method you prefer, the trick is to be disciplined in the way that you use them and to build them into your routine.

Review and update your list first thing each morning. It helps to set you up for the day, increasing your sense of purpose and control. You could add writing the list into an early morning anchor point routine.

If you prefer to handwrite your lists, you can decide whether to buy a ready-made to-do pad, find a printable template online, or just draw lines on a page. Most students find it helpful to separate different areas of their lives but still like to see everything that needs to be done on one sheet of paper. They just cross a line through each item to show when it is done. This is very helpful when students are juggling their studies with part-time work.

This kind of straightforward list works best if it is done daily:

Today's to-do list	
College	**Work**
Watch yesterday's lecture	Swap early shift with someone
Review sources for assignment	Order new staff uniform
Check the location for the seminar	
Personal	
Book dentist	
Order birthday gift for Sam	

Here's a blank daily to-do list you can try if you like.

Today's to-do list	
School/college/university	Work

Personal

More complicated listing methods can include deadlines and/or prioritizing systems. These tend to work better for slightly longer-term planning. There are some examples in the next section.

Digital list-making

If you prefer digital listing, there are many different apps you can try, such as 'TickTick' and '2Do'. More advanced apps can often change your meeting/lecture notes into to-do lists (like OneNote and Evernote). These (and many others) can sync with different systems, calendars and social media. You will get reminders as notifications. You can prioritize, tag and set sub-tasks which means you can still structure your list in a way that can separate different roles in your life.

Non-linear to-do lists

Some neurodivergent students do not think in linear ways at all and are naturally averse to lists. You can recreate all of these ideas using mind maps too. Have a look at this example; you will see the student has used dotted lines to show when actions are related to (or dependent upon) each other. Some find this very helpful.

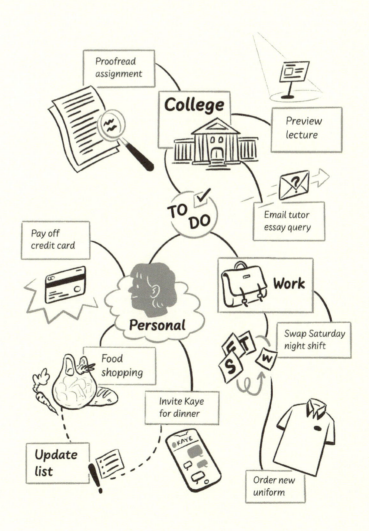

Another way of making a more creative to-do list is to write each of your action points on to individual sticky notes. You can pop them all up on to a wall (or fridge) in whatever shape you like. It can be quite satisfying to physically remove, screw up and throw away individual sticky notes when you have completed a task. Having moveable notes also allows you to reprioritize them easily by sticking them in a different order – that can be very handy. There are some other ideas about prioritizing your list items in the next few paragraphs.

Prioritizing your list items

Sometimes we simply have too many things on our list. This can happen despite your best attempts and can become a huge barrier to getting anything done at all. It might all feel insurmountable, which can be paralysing.

There is a variety of different strategies that you can try to help you break down your tasks and prioritize your time more effectively. Some different methods are described below.

 Try to think of nibbling away at your list, a bit like a squirrel. If you take little, regular bites, it will soon reduce in size.

Using the ABC method

This method was first developed by Alan Lakein[3] in the 1970s. It attaches a priority status to your things to do, with A being the most important and C being the least. You can also think of this as 'must do', 'should do' or 'could do'. Here is an example:

To do	ABC	
Final read of assignment and submit by noon	A	must
Make notes on yesterday's seminar	B	should
Book doctor's appointment	A	must
Choose and order new trainers	C	could
Go for a run	B	should

Or in an alternative column layout (which I think is clearer):

Today I...

Must	Should	Could
Final read of assignment and submit by noon	Make notes on yesterday's seminar	Choose and order new trainers
Book doctor's appointment	Go for a run	

 Here's a blank must, could, should table for you to try.

Must	Should	Could
Example: submit essay	*Pre-read lecture notes for tomorrow*	*Call Jen for a chat*

Prioritizing your lists: high medium low method

Here you add a kind of prioritization code to the items on your list: H for high, M for medium and L for low.

The first item listed might not necessarily be the highest priority and the date due is not always related to the level of priority. Some students hate this because it feels counterintuitive, but it recognizes that sometimes the most recent thing that has come up might just be the most important.

Here's an example:

Date: Monday 1st			
	To do	Due by	Priority H, M, L
1	Email professor with planning question	Wednesday 3rd	M
2	Book room in library for group discussion task	Tuesday 2nd	M
3	Find sources for next assignment	Friday 5th	H
4	Check rescheduled seminar date	Monday 8th	L
5	Finalize dissertation question	Friday 5th	H
6	Book doctor's appointment	NOW	H
Notes			

Prioritizing your lists: RAG method

If you like colour coding, you can RAG-rate your priorities instead. RAG stands for red, amber, green. Red indicates 'do now', amber indicates 'need to do soon' and green indicates 'there is no particular rush'.

 You can write your list in columns headed red, amber, green, or just use highlighter pens to colour code different items on any style of list.

Prioritizing using the Eisenhower matrix

This is a good method for slightly longer-term planning and prioritization. It's based on the ideas of former US president Eisenhower, who evaluated problems according to their urgency and importance.

This is a very useful tool, which can really help you to understand what you need to do now, and what can wait. It is based on a square with four quadrants where you can write in your things to do based on how important or urgent you think they are.

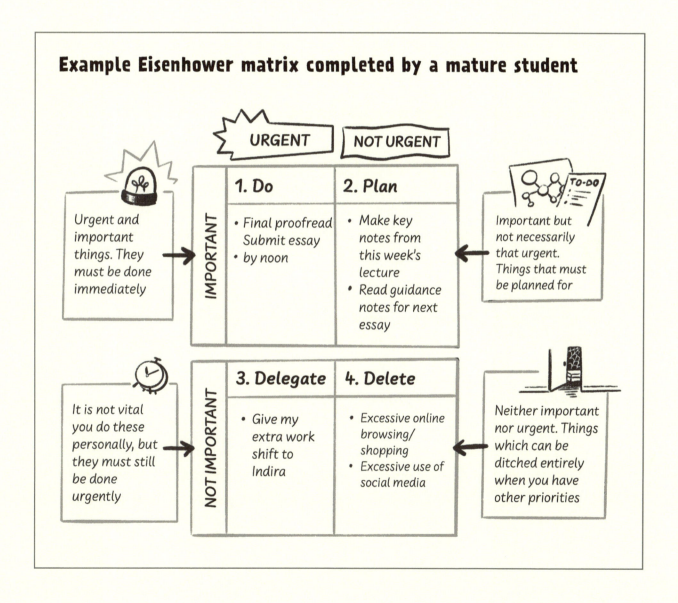

Example Eisenhower matrix completed by a mature student

Here's a blank template based on the Eisenhower matrix for you to use.

Do now (urgent and important)	Plan (important but not urgent)
Delegate (urgent but not important for you to do yourself)	Delete (not urgent, not important)

Using smart speakers, alarms and timers

Most students have smartphones and/or speakers which have alarms and timers. These can be very useful when studying. Here are some ways you could use them:

* Set an alarm to remind you to move every hour, or to remember to eat (if that's something that you are likely to forget).

* Set a series of reminders on your smart speaker to prompt you to think about your next assignment. Here you would look at your yearly planner and ask your speaker to remind you **a week before** each deadline that it is coming up.

* Set reminders for any regular medication you need to take.

 A quick note: Some people don't like being told what to do by machines. I can get quite cross with my own smart speaker if she starts ordering me around, even if I have asked her to! You can try phrasing your reminders differently. Instead of saying 'Submit my assignment today', you might say 'My physics assignment is due today'. That way, it is less of a command and more of a description of an event, so it feels less like being nagged.

Using an imaginary filing cabinet

This is more unusual, but some students really like it, particularly if they have strong imaginations. It is the idea of having a make-believe filing cabinet in your head. This is how it works:

* First, imagine an old-fashioned paper filing system, where important information is stored inside drawers.

* Each drawer has cardboard pockets for hanging files with little labels.

* Each of these labels has a date written on it.

* You can decide that you will deal with a problem or issue on a given date.

* You can put your problem or issue into a folder in your mental filing cabinet under that date.

* You close the drawer until that date.

* You can also transfer that mental date into your physical or digital calendar. This way if the problem or issue pops into your mind, you can remind yourself that you will be dealing with it on another day.

It's important to remember that this is a way of managing your priorities, not of continually kicking an issue that you don't want to deal with further down the road! This helps when you are feeling stressed and worried about something over which you have little control.

Using an imaginary filing cabinet: an example

Damien is awaiting the outcome of a marking appeal and is spending a huge amount of time worrying about what will happen, running through different scenarios in his mind. Using his mental filing cabinet, he's able to remind himself that he will be thinking about this on the date the appeal is to be decided, and not before.

This is also a way of avoiding procrastination by distraction, which we'll look at in more detail in Chapter 4.

Next, we're going to look at how to organize your real materials rather than imaginary ones!

Organizing your materials

There is a multitude of different ways of organizing your materials. Having a good system in place helps you find information quickly and easily. This saves time and stress when you are trying to write assignments or revise for tests.

> *'Materials' refers to all the information you collect when you are studying, for example, texts, videos, readings, handouts and notes.*

One tried and tested way of organizing your materials is to use some form of coding system, and this can work well both with analogue or digital methods.

 Coding systems are likely to work particularly well for you if you can easily recognize and match patterns.

Using coding systems

The most straightforward method of coding is to use colour to help you identify quickly which topic or module you are looking at. You can do the following:

* Colour code all your physical or digital folders according to subject.
* Follow this colour code throughout all of your personal organization strategies.

That means using matching colours on your wall planner (or digital planner) for classes and deadlines.

* Choose colours which are somehow meaningful for you as this helps you to make mental links. For example, you might choose green for environmental studies.

 High school students sometimes shade their timetables with pencils that match the colours of the exercise books they are using in each lesson. This can help them quickly pack the right books in the morning.

Colour coding example

A student is studying the topic of jurisprudence as part of a law course. Everything to do with jurisprudence will be coded in purple. They have chosen purple because they always think that jurisprudence sounds a bit like 'prunes', and prunes are a purple colour. It also makes them smile!

However, some students find many different colours a little jarring. If this applies to you, you can still use visual cues to help you organize your materials. It is about playing to your strengths.

You might choose to identify a particular symbol or shape with a topic area or module. For example, everything related to the topic of social class is coded with a circle. You might even use images in the same way, but these do need to be consistent.

 The Noun Project[4] is a good source of simplified black-and-white images (patterns, shapes and physical objects).

You can also use coding more specifically to help you identify themes or source material which might be relevant to a particular topic or assignment. Students who need to complete a dissertation can find this particularly helpful as these usually include literature reviews that are often structured thematically. Such students can give each of their proposed themes a colour and then choose to tag source material with the matching colour according to their identified themes.

> **Case study: using coding in practice**
>
> Valeria is studying a programme with an important end-of-semester assignment. It is worth 60 per cent of the marks, so she needs to do well.
>
> The question is released at the start of the semester. Valeria reads this carefully, thinking about the contents she will need to include.
>
> Then, for the rest of the semester, every time she comes across something which might be useful for the assignment, she puts a small star beside it.
>
> At the end of the semester, she can go through her notes and see all of the stars. This helps to narrow down the process of finding good source information, reducing her time and stress levels.

Organizing your other 'stuff'

How to avoid losing things

Maybe you find that you often lose things, particularly inside your home. It's a really common experience among my students and causes lots of stress. It can also make them late for classes as they can't leave home on time because of being unable to locate some vital item like their keys.

Here are a few strategies you could try to help:

* Find a plate or tray. Put this somewhere near the exit to your home. Put all of your vital items on it every time you arrive home.

* Say aloud where you are putting your items: 'I am putting my keys on the kitchen table.' This helps to embed the placement into your memory.

* Count the number of important items you need to take out with you: keys, phone, wallet. Three things. It enables you to check that you have those three before you exit.

* Create a visual checklist by your door – items that you should not leave without (a series of printed photos stuck up on the door works well).

* Put physical reminders in obvious places. For example, if you need to remember to take your reading glasses to college, put your glasses case by the front door. Likewise, you can put your regular medication next to your breakfast cereal in the cupboard as long as that's safe to do so – don't do this if there are children about!

* Set up a smart speaker routine so that it reminds you what you need to take with you on the days you have classes. Set it to ask you 20 minutes before you are due to leave: 'Do you have your keys, your wallet, your bus pass and your laptop?'

* Use the method of loci to create a mental checklist of items (look at Chapter 8 for details).

* Attach 'finding' tech to your most important things. You can buy tags to put in bags and on keys. For example, I have a terrible track record of losing keys. My partner put a (cheap) tag on my keys and in a drawer. If I press the drawer tag, my keys whistle to me and I just follow the noise.

* If this all feels a bit too organized for you, you can try putting a box in every room for 'important stuff'. Toss your bank card in there once you have made that purchase. It reduces the number of places you have to look when you can't find it next time!

How to avoid getting physically lost

This can be a big hurdle for many students, particularly those with dyspraxia in their profiles, where having difficulties with sense of direction is commonplace. This makes unfamiliar environments challenging. Navigating around college or university is particularly tricky for new students. Understandably, this can be anxiety inducing.

Using technology can be very helpful. However, saying, 'use Google Maps' is not always useful as we can't all orientate ourselves well in space (I certainly can't). There might also be safety concerns in some areas and it can be unwise to walk around staring at expensive smartphones in our hands.

Here are some tips you might like to try:

* If you find the idea of working out where you need to get to a bit overwhelming, try using AI to help. You can type 'How can I get from [name of place] to [name of place]?' and it will give you a list of different options using both public and private transport. If you want to narrow it down, just be more specific, so add: 'by train' etc. It will need checking but can be a very good jumping-off point to start with.

* Check out your route beforehand. If possible, walk it. Note important waymarks and take photos of them. Try to make mental links with the visual clues. For example, note there is a pub on the corner where you need to turn left. Even better if it is called 'The Lion', as this can become 'left for lion'! Take a picture of the pub with your phone. It helps if the link is a bit ridiculous as our brains tend to take note of things which are out of the ordinary.

* If you can't walk the route, you can use Google Maps on Street View to help you virtually do the same thing. Again, try looking for waymarks such as buildings.

* Take photos generally. If you leave your car in a car park, take a picture of where it is. Also, take a photo of what you can see from where it is parked. This is very helpful in giant car parks as it helps you narrow down the area more quickly. If losing your car is a 'thing' and you have the funds for more expensive tech, you can buy tags which you can leave in your car and track using your phone.

- Many organizations have video tours of their sites available online. If you are going somewhere new, always check to see if there is a tour that you can watch.

- If you find that you are getting lost within buildings, take photos of the exit and entrance corridors, particularly anything significant, like a painting next to the exit corridor. Again, you are trying to make mental links.

- Keep the contact details of the person you are going to see or the helpdesk number if you are visiting a public building. If you are stuck, you can ask for directions. Ask them to text (or email) them to you rather than explaining over the phone. It can be very hard on your working memory to try to remember all those 'go left, then right, then take the third left' instructions when they are given verbally and you aren't able to write them down!

- If you have a fear of getting lost, you might like to give yourself a 'familiar place' to retreat to. For example, a student living in London might know their way home from Oxford Circus. They know if they can get there, they will be fine.

- Leave plenty of extra time. Assume that you will get lost and that you might need to backtrack on yourself.

Now that you have many different ideas about how to organize every aspect of your study life, it's time to think about tackling anything else that might be stopping you from learning. That's what we'll look at in the next chapter.

Let's recap

In this chapter we have covered:

- how to organize your space
- how to organize your time using layers of planning (yearly, monthly/weekly, daily)
- importance of routine and rhythm
- time management strategies
- prioritizing methods
- organizing your materials using coding
- organizing other things (tips to avoid losing 'stuff' or getting lost).

 Key takeaway points from this chapter

- Take time at the start of the year to organize your diary or planner. Transferring deadlines now will save heartache later.
- Break your time down into manageable chunks.
- Write to-do lists.

Chapter 4

OVERCOMING BARRIERS TO LEARNING

Avoiding Procrastination

Introduction

The first point to make is to say that I **really** dislike the word 'procrastination' when it's applied to neurodivergent students! That's because it has connotations of being lazy and, in my experience, neurodivergent students are very far from that. However, I have used it here because it is a term which is easily understood and widely used. That said, it is **much** better to think about this as overcoming those barriers which stop you from getting things done. In this chapter we are going to look at some of the most common barriers students have told me they typically face, and what you can do to overcome them. We will cover:

* difficulty transitioning between activities
* experiencing decision paralysis or overwhelm when having to make a decision
* maintaining focus.

But first, we are going to start thinking about your own situation and any barriers that you can identify right now.

Reflecting on what's stopping you

This reflection is the first thing you can do. You can write a list of what's stopping you and then write a corresponding list of steps you can take to overcome this. You could put this on a notice board near your desk to help yourself when you are feeling 'stuck'.

 Don't try to write this list when you are already feeling 'stuck'. Write it on a good day when you are feeling positive about your studies. It will come in useful later!

Your list might look a bit like the one below (you can copy this list too, if it helps).

Barrier	Things that might help
Am I hungry, thirsty or tired?	This is the first question you should ask yourself. If so, eat, drink or nap! You must attend to your basic needs first before you try to study.
I don't understand the question.	Check class or lecture notes. Ask a friend. Email my tutor and ask for help.
I am confused by the topic.	Read over the class notes again. Try watching some YouTube clips (check if these are from reputable sources like other colleges or universities). Ask a friend. Email my tutor and ask for help.

I am convinced I will fail anyway, so there's no point.	Look back at your previous work. First, note down the things you did well. Then, check your feedback carefully and write a list of the things you can do to improve. Tick these off as you incorporate the feedback into your next piece of work. It will feel like an achievement (because it is).
I'm bored.	Set yourself a small target, e.g., I will write a 15-minute essay plan, then I will have a 5-minute break. If you have ADHD in your profile, you may have a lower boredom threshold and so must find something which is more stimulating to be able to continue. You could try: • introducing some element of competition/trying to gamify the task, e.g., 'Can you beat the clock?' • introducing things that you enjoy and find rewarding into the process, e.g., if you are creative, you could make a beautiful booklet for your revision, using drawings and mind maps.
I don't know how to start.	1. A quick trick is to turn an essay question into a statement and start writing. So, 'Discuss the role of women in Shakespeare's *King Lear*' becomes 'This essay will discuss the role of women in Shakespeare's *King Lear*.' That's often enough to get you going. 2. Discuss your ideas with someone else and record the conversation (with their permission). Listen back and use this to prompt your writing. 3. Use speech-to-text. This works well if your verbal skills are stronger than your written ones.
I just can't focus on the reading.	Try to work out how you *feel* about the source. It might help you feel more connected to the subject and more engaged. Write down your ideas. You can use strong language if it helps you – this is only for you! Do you think it's a load of rubbish? Do you like the writing style?

cont.

Barrier	Things that might help
There's too much to do so I'm feeling overwhelmed.	Try using one of the prioritization strategies listed later in this chapter. Give yourself 'just three things' to do. Write each one on a sticky note. Put them up where you can see them. Throw each one away as you complete the task. These should be short, doable things like 'proofread my introduction', **not** 'write my assignment'! Remember, mood affects behaviour. If you feel stressed or anxious, try doing a short activity that you find calming. If you are feeling sluggish, do something active. This could be as straightforward as a walk around the block. Use your 'joyful things' list (see Chapter 2 for an example).
I am only interested in one particular thing at the moment – my 'special interest'.	This is tricky because sometimes your 'special interest' might feel like an itch that just needs to be scratched so it's impossible to focus on anything else. You could try doing the following: 1. Give yourself a set time in the day (and a time limit) to 'scratch that itch'. You'll need to experiment. Doing it first thing might work, as long as you are not tempted to spend the rest of the day on it! The end of the day might be better but **only** if waiting for that doesn't mean you can't focus. 2. Distract yourself with other activities (again, give yourself a time limit). 3. Try to develop a range of different 'special interests' so that you can switch to a different one if you feel that one is taking over too much (I appreciate this can be easier said than done).

On the other hand, students sometimes tell me that once they get going on something they can find it hard to stop! This means that transitioning between activities can be tricky and they might become 'stuck' in one area. Here are some ideas you might try if this applies to you.

Managing transitions between activities

'Now and next'

Use the 'now and next' strategy we discussed earlier when talking about avoiding overwhelm. If you know you tend to find it difficult to swap between tasks, write yourself a list of 'what I will do now' and 'what I will do next'. If you like, you can set yourself a timer so that you can move on to the 'next' column at a given time. Remember these should be 'small' things, so they feel like short, doable tasks. For example, 'Now I will read the assignment guidance through once' and 'Next I will use a highlighter to mark key instructions'.

Physically differentiate between tasks

It can help to physically differentiate between tasks so that you are putting one thing away and starting another. That's harder in a digital world.

 Think about having different folders for your notes, or even using different systems for different activities. In my own life, I use Google for one of my jobs and Microsoft for another. That helps me work out where I am, and what I should be doing!

Using a visual timer

This comes with a caveat as some people would find this too stressful and would be permanently watching it, feeling pressurized to complete a task. You can find things like digital egg timers online, which can be quite nice to watch drain. Again, you would need to experiment to see if this works for you.

Link a regular transition with some kind of sensory signal

> For example, if you are trying to ensure that you eat lunch at 1pm, you could set up your smart speaker to play a tune at 1pm every day. You could try something similar at bedtime. Equally, you might always like to listen to the sounds of the rainforest when you are studying. If you play that on your headphones, your mind and body will begin to recognize, 'Ah, it's study time'. If tastes or smells are very vivid for you, you can try using something edible or perfumed instead; for example, some students like to chew when they are studying.

However, even studying at all can be very difficult if you have a larger problem or decision which is 'shouting' at you from the sidelines, making it impossible for you to get going with your work. So, let's have a look at some ways to help with that next.

Decision-making and problem-solving ideas

Sometimes you will need to make a decision to be able to get on with your studies. For example, you might have to choose a dissertation topic, pick your next module or decide which essay question to do from a list of five. Equally, you might find that you have an insurmountable problem that you just can't find a way of resolving.

This can be very difficult if you might naturally tend to see the bigger picture. You may worry that you will get the decision wrong, or that you will miss something vital if you choose one pathway over another.

Getting your thoughts out of your mind using some kind of objective method can be helpful here. Therefore, I have listed some common strategies that you might like to try. We're focused on study skills here, but the following techniques can also work for other life decisions, such as which internships to apply for or what jobs to consider.

Consider the positives and negatives

This is very straightforward. You simply list the positives of taking a particular course of action in a column on one side of the page, and the negatives in a second column. Comparing the length of these two lists can help you to decide which is the 'right' thing for you to do.

This works best for simple problems.

SWOT analysis

SWOT stands for strengths, weaknesses, opportunities and threats. This method started as a business management tool[1] but can be used more widely. It's useful as it can help you to take a 'snapshot' of the situation in the round. Many of my students really like it because it is a bit more nuanced and considers external factors which might be out of your control.

Example SWOT for a student trying to decide whether to travel abroad for a period of study

Strengths (internal – I have some influence over these things)	Weaknesses (internal – I have some influence over these things)
1. Strengthens subject knowledge	1. Might miss family and the dog
2. Enjoying a new environment – interesting food and culture	2. Increased anxiety for a while as everything is new
3. Being with other people who share my passion for the subject	3. Time and stress of organizing it all
Opportunities (external – these are more outside my control)	**Threats (external – these are more outside my control)**
1. Good for my CV when I leave uni	1. Expensive (rent, travel, living costs)
2. Helpful contacts made?	2. Need to find another part-time job when I get back

As you can see from this example, the decision can be finely balanced and the 'right' path to take might not be immediately clear. If this happens, then I would say you should go back through your list and highlight the things that are the most important to you. For example, this student might feel that strengthening their subject knowledge and being with like-minded people is **the** most important thing to them in the world. That will give more weight to the strengths. Another student might have very tight finances and no means of external support. The fact that travelling abroad is so expensive might be enough to make them decide not to go. As an aside – if I were supporting that particular student, I would tell them to go to their university and see if any bursaries or other financial support is available before they decide they can't go!

The DECIDE decision-making model

DECIDE is an acronym for the steps you can take in the decision-making process. There are actually several different decision-making models which use the same DECIDE acronym! I have chosen this particular model[2] as it has a section which asks you to consider the influence of your own values. That's because over the years I have found that many neurodivergent people have a strong sense of what feels morally right or wrong, so incorporating these feelings into decision-making feels appropriate to me. Have a look at the example to see how it works.

An example from a psychology student

D	Define the decision	I need to pick between two different pathways for my psychology degree next year.
E	Explore the different options	Look at both pathways in depth. Highlight the areas I find most interesting in both pathways.
C	Consider the consequences	Is one pathway more appropriate for the eventual career I would like to do? Is one pathway more interesting to me?
I	Identify your values	Does one pathway 'fit' better with my value system and outlook on life?
D	Decide and act	Take all of the above into consideration and complete the electronic choice form!
E	Evaluate the outcome	I won't be able to do this until I have started my course.

The three decision-making models above assume that you know what the problem is to start with. Sometimes, actually defining the issue and working out what decisions need to be considered can be very tricky. If you find yourself in that situation, you could try using the next technique.

A Study Skills Survival Guide for Neurodivergent Learners

Ishikawa diagram (a problem-solving strategy)

This is a fishbone-shaped, cause-and-effect model which can help you to visualize the possible **causes** of a problem. It was first created by Kaoru Ishikawa,[3] an engineering professor at the University of Tokyo, as a quality improvement strategy. Like SWOT, this was originally intended as a business tool. You can still use it for other problems and it can be very good if you are working as a team on a problem-solving assignment or project.

This is how to use one:

* Put your problem on the right-hand side of your page in the fish head.

* Think about (or discuss, if you are in a group) the potential causes of the problem. Put these as the main bones (or branches) for your fish.

* Then look at each of these main bones and consider the question further – why might this be happening? Write your ideas as smaller bones (sub-branches).

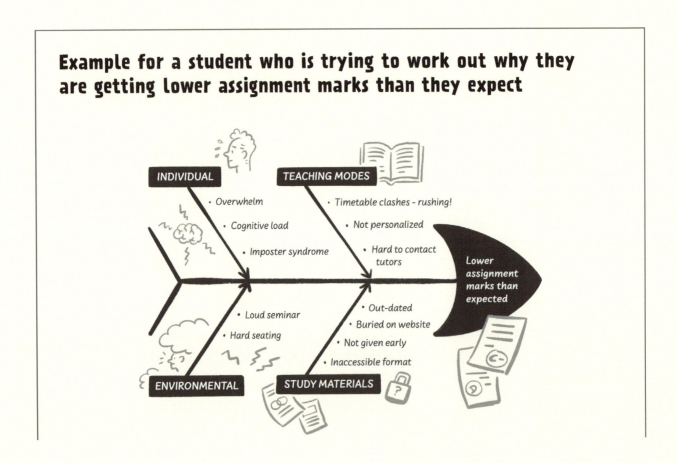

> The next stage for this student is to work out what they can **practically do** to resolve some of these causes. For example, they could ask their tutor to give them a copy of the study material for each lecture in advance and bring a cushion to sit on.

Deciding what you are working on and what needs to be done is, of course, an important step. However, once you start studying, it's not always easy to stay on track, particularly if you're doing something you don't find very interesting. So, the next section looks at some ways to manage this.

Maintaining focus once you are studying

Hopefully, you are now at the point where you are ready to sit down and study. However, maintaining focus is not always easy, so here are some other ideas to help with this.

Mirroring

Try studying alongside others. There is increasing research which discusses the positive role of 'mirroring'[4] when we look at behaviour. This is the idea that we tend to copy the behaviours of those who are around us. Sometimes this is also known as body-doubling and it can be helpful for study. It means many students find that being in a space with others who are also working quietly and studiously helps them to do the same.

You might even be able to identify a friend who will act as a **study buddy** to work alongside you. If you are a bit sceptical about mirroring, I challenge you to try it! A library is a good, safe place to experiment with this strategy.

> *If you are using a study buddy, make sure that they are as committed to the task as you are, otherwise they could be a source of distraction!*

Study groups

Consider creating a study group as these can work incredibly effectively. Be warned, these need a structured agenda and a clear timeframe for each meeting so that you are not tempted to just chat! You will find more about using study groups for revision in Chapter 8 'Achieving Your Goals in Exams'.

Using a doodle box

Doodling can really help some neurodivergent students concentrate, particularly if they like to keep their hands busy or find it harder to focus when they have to listen for longer periods.[5]

You might already be a 'doodler' without recognizing this as a strategy which you've found naturally helpful! Perhaps there's a favourite kind of doodle that you draw repeatedly. This repetition can help your brain form memories and associate the doodles with recall. It can also be soothing from a sensory perspective, particularly if your pen glides easily along the paper or your tablet screen. However, we don't want your doodles to take over the whole page or become your main focus, which is where creating a 'doodle box' comes in.

You draw yourself a section on your page or tablet screen, which you designate for doodling. You can choose different colours for different subjects, or even have a particular kind of repeating shape or pattern which you associate with certain types of course material. Having this specific space to doodle in can be a very useful focusing tool when you are watching previously recorded lectures or attending face-to-face tutorials.

A quick note – if you are doodling to help you focus when attending classes, you can let your teachers know in advance. Sometimes they can mistake doodling for daydreaming or inattentiveness. We'll look more at managing in class in Chapter 5.

What to try when you find yourself procrastinating

There will be times when, despite all your best efforts, you still find that you are stuck in that 'procrastination zone', so we'll end this chapter with this list of things you can try to help yourself move forward.

* Break it down. If a task feels insurmountable, it can really help to reduce it into smaller chunks. 'Start my assignment' feels huge, but 'Read the task guidance and highlight the key steps I need to take' feels much more specific and doable.

* Change activity. Sometimes allowing yourself to do something different for a few minutes will be enough to give your brain a break and allow it to refocus.

* Challenge yourself. Give yourself five minutes to jot down absolutely everything you know about the topic or question you are working on. It doesn't matter what order the information is in or how informally you write. Students often surprise themselves with how much they know and that is motivating in itself!

* Talk it through. You can tell someone else, or your smartphone, what you are writing about. Record this (with permission) and play it back to spark your ideas.

* Change environment. Try working in another room or space.

* Move. Stand up, do some stretches and have a walk around for a few minutes.

* Play some energizing music.

* Find an accountability buddy. This doesn't work for everyone, but I have seen it work very well, particularly for those with ADHD in their profiles. Pick someone in your class and agree that you will try to keep each other on track. You can set regular progress 'checking-in' times. This could be a message every Monday morning to tell each other where you are up to.

* Just leave it entirely and do something completely different. That might sound

counterintuitive, but if you are totally stuck, there's no point in sitting looking at a blank screen, probably feeling bad about yourself. There is almost certainly something else that you could be usefully doing, even if that's washing up or going food shopping. If you can find a 'useful' task to do, it will make you feel better about doing it. It also means you won't have to do it later and that should give you more time for studying when you are in a better place to do so!

We've covered quite a bit about how to manage your own learning, but that can be quite a bit trickier when you are doing that in a class or group environment. We'll look at different ways of managing in class in the next chapter.

 Let's recap

In this chapter we have covered:

- reflecting on barriers to learning and ways to overcome them
- managing transitions between activities
- decision-making and problem-solving ideas
- maintaining focus when studying
- what to do if you find yourself in a 'procrastination zone'.

 Key takeaway points from this chapter

- Working out what your personal barriers to learning are is a good place to start.
- Switching activities is generally a good plan if you find yourself 'stuck' and unable to focus.
- Using decision-making tools or problem-solving strategies can help to externalize things and so help you feel more objective about moving forward.

Chapter 5

MANAGING IN CLASS AND NOTE-TAKING IN LECTURES

There are definitely barriers when it comes to studying in groups. Whether you are in school, college or university, each setting has its own set of challenges. Since the Covid-19 pandemic, some colleges and universities are also offering at least some of their lectures online, which can also prove tricky.

Perhaps the issue that most students raise with me is that of being able to maintain focus and reduce overwhelm, so this is where we will start.

Strategies for maintaining focus and reducing overwhelm

Here is a list of common issues and strategies that you could try to help.

Issue	Possible strategy	Comment
I can't keep up with what is being said and I miss information.	Ask for copies of the lecture notes/slides beforehand, so you can pre-read and look up any unfamiliar vocabulary or terminology.	This is usually considered a reasonable adjustment (accommodation) so should be easily provided.
	Record the class – play it back afterwards.	You must obtain permission to do this (usually from the teacher **and** the class).
	Use professional note-taking software or apps which will record and note the content.	Software can be expensive and, again, you need permission. It is also quite passive and might mean that you do not necessarily absorb all of the content. However, it does allow you to go back through the notes after the lecture.
	Find a trusted peer and ask if you can copy their notes.	This is free, but the quality is not always guaranteed.
	Take active notes using one of the strategies described below.	This is more likely to keep your brain engaged. Try listening for keywords and phrases. Have a question in mind before you enter the class. What is it that you need to know?
I find it really hard to keep focused on the speaker for the whole class and my mind tends to drift away on to other things.	Find something quiet to fiddle with. You can buy a wide range of 'fiddle toys' (like squishy balls, etc.) or you can find something from home.	Your brain might actually need some form of distraction to stay alert, particularly if you have ADHD in your profile. Try to play to your sensory preferences here, so if you enjoy stretchy things, choose something stretchy. Maybe switch colours for your notes, or change the method of your note-taking for a while (switch to mind maps).
	Use a doodle box.	Look back at the previous chapter for how doodling can help you maintain focus.

	Take regular short breaks.	Some lectures can be over two hours long! You might need to agree on breaks beforehand. Ensure that you have a walk around and a bit of a stretch in your breaks.
	Reduce distractions.	Think about your sight line. Are you next to a window? Try to position yourself so that you have minimal visual distractions.
The environment itself is really uncomfortable for me. It's noisy and bright. The chairs are too hard.	Ensure that you can 'escape'. Find a seat which is on the end of a row, ideally near the exit – get agreement that this will always be 'your' seat. Use an inflatable cushion (the travel/camping ones are good) or get a wobble cushion/wedge for your class chair (find them online or via your educational institution's additional needs team). Wear dark glasses to help with glare. Use in-ear headphones or in-ear noisereduction devices to reduce sound during group activities.	If you are chatty, avoid sitting next to someone similar, otherwise you will distract each other.
I'm too worried about something else to focus.	Write your worry down on a sticky note or piece of paper and put it in your pocket.	This 'saves' your worry, for later. Tell yourself that now is not the time to be thinking about it (I realise that is easier said than done but it's worth a try).

Note-taking skills and strategies

One of the underpinning skills for successful study is the ability to take good, clear, succinct and accurate notes. These form the basis of your essay writing and mean you can avoid wasting time trawling through reams of information if you can refer straight back to your notes.

However, often students tell me that taking notes during classes is **very** difficult. That's because many neurodivergent people have differences in the way their working memory can manipulate and process information. This can make it tricky to listen to new material, hold that in your head, manipulate it and then produce a shortened form in the way of notes. All of this has to happen while trying to absorb the next point the speaker is making. If this is combined with an uncomfortable environment and a teacher who may be difficult to hear…well, it's no wonder note-taking can be a real challenge!

However, there are many different note-taking methods and an increasing range of digital tools which can help, some of which are summarized below.

 Ask your tutor or teacher for a copy of their notes/slides before the class. Skim read these before the lecture. Look up any unfamiliar words beforehand.

Digital note-taking

In its simplest form, digital note-taking can be as basic as using a stylus to write your notes on a tablet device. This has advantages in terms of being able to keep your information in one place. You can have multiple folders on one device, which you can colour code according to topic or subject. You can use different colours while you are writing to highlight different ideas and thoughts. This can also help to keep your writing feeling 'fresh'.

You might also consider using one of the many note-taking/organizing apps which are now available. There are too many for me to list here, but two commonly used ones are Microsoft OneNote and Evernote. Generally, these kinds of apps allow you to:

* upload, scan and clip text from different sources
* draw and write on to documents using your finger or stylus
* record (and upload) audio clips and videos
* take free-form notes, or use preloaded note-taking templates
* tag information
* create reminders and to-do lists.

Once you get used to them, they allow you to keep everything in one place and have your entire course content immediately at hand rather than in a series of folders on your desk at home. They also integrate with your calendar so can give you prompts and reminders about deadlines and appointments. To work well, you will need to have a smart tablet or screen on your laptop that works with a stylus and to be able to carry this around with you.

'Live' transcription note-taking technology

Many students like to use this tech to help reduce the load on their working memory, particularly during live lectures where pausing the discussion isn't an option. These apps will convert speech into text in real time.

It's an area which is evolving very quickly in response to the rapid development of language-learning-based AI. I hope this section will still be up to date by the time you get to read it, but I would advise you to do an internet search to double-check some of the features described, as the situation is constantly changing.

Two popular apps used by my students are Glean and Otter.ai (there are others available), and they are similarly priced. You can try the free basic versions first, to make sure that you like them. Then there will be either a time limit, or a transcription limit, which makes payment the only realistic option moving forward. Remember that you might also be able to obtain this software as part of a reasonable adjustment allowance, so do check with the team/person whose job it is to support you at school or university before you make a purchase.

They share these broadly similar abilities:

* They record every spoken word in face-to-face, online or pre-recorded lectures, typing the words on your screen in real time.

* They can convert audio and video files to text.

* They enable you to add notes or highlight certain points during live transcription.

* You can link and label information.

* You can upload linked information (like your tutor's slides).

They can generate an automatic outline/summary of key points. Be aware that having pages of transcription on its own is not necessarily helpful, particularly if you haven't actively engaged with note-taking, for example, by highlighting during live transcription. You will still need to go through the notes afterwards to ensure you have absorbed the key points and understood the material. This is one of the reasons that some students prefer to take their own notes. Others prefer the look and feel of paper notes, particularly if they have a form of visual stress, which makes looking at screens for long periods uncomfortable.

 Remember that you need permission to record others. This will usually be a reasonable adjustment (accommodation) so speak to the person in charge of additional needs if you encounter problems with this.

Other note-taking methods

The following section has seven different note-taking strategies for you to experiment with. Lots of them can be used with paper and pen as well as on digital devices, particularly if you have a tablet and stylus. Remember that different strategies might work better in different contexts, so it could be that you will find that you are switching between different methods – that's fine.

Cornell notes

This method was first introduced by an education professor working at Cornell University in the USA, Walter Pauk.[1] The university has some excellent videos which talk you through the method very clearly and, if you prefer to learn by watching, I would encourage you to look these up.[2]

It is a systematic approach which asks students to think about the lecture before, during and after it is held. It encourages you to think about what you want to get out of the class, what you have learned and what you still need to know. This means it is a very active way of note-taking which can help you to stay engaged with the topic.

Cornell notes is also available as a template on both OneNote and Evernote (and doubtless many other digital note-taking apps). The page is divided into three sections, with each section having a very deliberate function.

Class name and date	
Cue column	**Notes section**
Before class: Are there any questions you need answered today?	During class:
	Class contents are written here.
During class: Are there any 'aha!' moments – are there new links?	Use bullet points, lists, symbols, diagrams.
After class: what do you need to know next?	You do not need every detail. Just the main points.
Summary section	
At the end of class: Write a sentence or two with the key learning points from the class.	
Very useful for essay writing. You can look back at this section and quickly decide whether it will be useful for your writing. Don't skip this section!	

You can also put some kind of visual reminder or 'code' into your summary section if you already know that the class content will be useful for an assignment, for example, a star shape. That way, when you are looking back through your notes, you can immediately find the information you need.

Example from a student who has attended a lecture on study skills

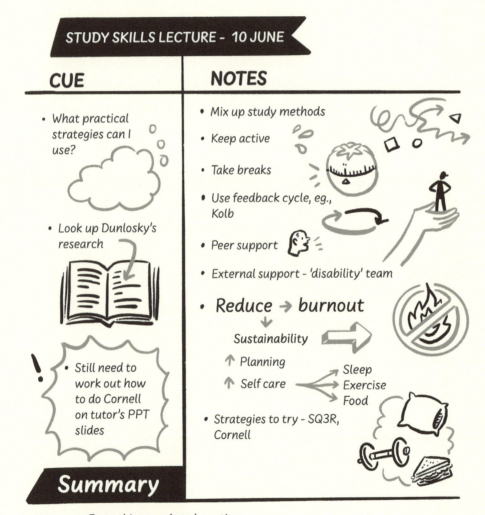

This method can take a bit of getting used to but can work very well. Sometimes you might find that you don't have time to complete the 'cue' column during the lecture. If so, don't worry. You can do this afterwards, or just put your 'Aha!' moments into your summary.

Students often worry that they will miss key information. One way of getting around this is to superimpose the Cornell structure over lecture slides. You can take your class slides and print them as notes pages (or print them as PDF if you are using digital methods). You then draw your Cornell sections on to those pages. That way, you keep your own notes with the original slides all in one place.

A final comment in this section about Cornell is to say that it's quite a flexible method. Therefore, although it was originally designed to be used to take lecture notes, many students also find that it works well for making notes when they are reading. That's because it's a very active way of engaging with any learning matter. They write the title of the document at the top of the page and use the 'sections' of the method in the same way. If you find this strategy useful for making lecture notes, you could experiment to see if it also helps you to read, understand and record key points in reading material.

 If you find drawing the sections irritating, you can buy ready-lined Cornell notebooks (easily found online). These are available in pastel colours too, which are great for visual stress.

Outlining note-taking strategy

Many people do this 'method' already, without actually realizing that they are doing it! It's a way of organizing information on a page using bullet points, which you expand upon beneath. You group your bullet points under main headings and subheadings so that you end up with a neat series of lists and sublists.

Here's an example:

ANATOMY OF SKIN (title)

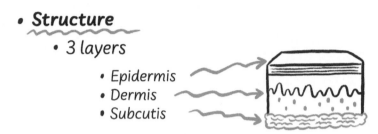

This is a straightforward method and can work well. The only disadvantage is that it can be quite hard to see how information links together as it's very linear.

Using boxes or flowcharts to link your ideas

With this method, you can draw boxes (or use the 'text box' digital feature) to separate your key points. It allows you to group important information and can make it easier to see key points.

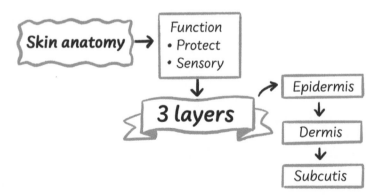

This is a useful method if you like to see how information is linked on a page. It also works well for processes (like in science), for subjects where chronology is important (like history), and where there are sets and subsets of information. It can be tricky to do in the middle of lectures until you get used to it.

Using mind maps

Mind maps can be very useful for note-taking, particularly as they help you to see all of the related ideas on one page. You can make them as basic, or beautiful, as you like. Some students like to colourcode their maps so that each main theme or idea is represented in its own hue.

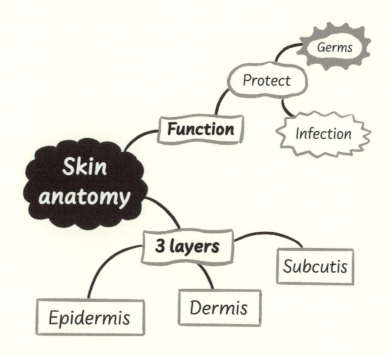

The sentence method

A caveat at the start: This method requires two stages and so can be time consuming! However, I have included it as you might find it useful if you happen to attend classes where the ideas aren't expressed in a very organized way, or the tutor speaks too quickly for you to be able to group your thoughts.

This is how it works:

* **Stage one:** simply list each new point made on a new line as the class progresses, without attempting to sort or link information.

* **Stage two:** sort your list into grouped ideas. This usually requires some rewriting.

As you need to repeat information here, it can help solidify this into your memory. If you are someone who doesn't mind spending a bit of extra time rewriting, this method could work for you.

 You can mix these methods. Some strategies suit different contexts. For example, you might use mind mapping to study an English literature course (because often works are discussed thematically) but boxes to note during science.

Using voice notes

If you find that listening to information is the best way for you to remember it, you can try recording your own voice notes. This works best when you are making your own notes at home (say, from textbooks), rather than in classes, just because it can be disruptive to others. You can then listen back as often as you like.

Note-taking for numerical/problem-based subjects – using T-notes

Students working in subjects which are number-based like maths, physics and engineering often tell me that the methods described above aren't suitable for them. Elvis Clark and Archie Davis[3] devised the T-note method which is a variation on the Cornell strategy. This can work much better for describing equations or maths methods.

To do this, just draw T-shaped lines to divide your page, creating three areas for your information. This makes things nice and easy to see, so it's very helpful if you need to recap or revise a topic. You can also take your lecture slides and superimpose your T-note structure by physically drawing lines on them, either digitally or by printing them out. Many students like to do this as it helps them to keep all of the relevant information together.

Here's how T-notes work:

Title of topic or equation (date of class etc.)	
Problem	**Solution**
Write down the equation, formula and example of the problem.	Give your explanation.
	Write down any steps you have taken.
	Break it down into clear stages so that you can use the same approach again.

This chapter has covered a lot about managing in class, from ways of maintaining focus to the very practical strategies that can be used when you are taking notes. As this book progresses we'll start to think about how you can convert your learning from lectures, readings and notes into assignments and achieve your goals in exams. We'll start with reading skills in the next chapter.

Let's recap

In this chapter we have covered:

- strategies for maintaining focus and reducing overwhelm
- note-taking skills and strategies:
    - digital note-taking technology
    - live transcription technology
    - Cornell notes
    - outlining strategy
    - using boxes and flowcharts
    - using mind maps
    - the sentence method
    - using voice notes
    - T-notes.

 Key takeaway points from this chapter

- Try to ensure that you are physically comfortable.
- Try out some of the strategies in the table at the beginning of the chapter.
- Note-taking strategies can be very helpful but take a bit of getting used to.
- Think about using tech to help.
- Don't give up! Once you find a strategy that you like, you can use it for life.

Chapter 6

READING AND UNDERSTANDING SOURCE MATERIAL

Introduction

Almost every neurodivergent student I work with finds it difficult to digest large volumes of text. They often tell me that while they **can** physically read the information, they do not feel that it is 'going in'. This means they end up rereading multiple times to try to make sense of the work, which is tiring, frustrating and time consuming. Here are some quick tips for you to start with.

Quick tips:

- **Reading needs to be active.** Do not expect to be able to sit still and passively absorb information. This just doesn't work. This is why the strategies in this section rely on a degree of self-interrogation. To help keep your brain engaged with the topic you need to be questioning both your own knowledge and the text.

- **Break up your reading time** into smaller chunks to make it more manageable. No one can read and retain huge chunks of information in one sitting.

- **Choose your most awake/alert** times to do the majority of your reading.

Skimming and scanning skills are considered essential for efficient reading, so it is worth talking about these at the outset before we move on to look at specific strategies.

Skimming

Skimming a text is to read quickly to get the main points, skipping over the details.

It is used to quickly identify the main ideas (the gist) of a text. It is generally done at a speed three to four times faster than normal reading. People often skim when they have lots of material to read in a limited amount of time.

It's useful to skim to:

* preview a passage before reading it in detail

* refresh understanding of a passage after it has been read in detail.

It is also helpful when exploring other resources, such as the internet, dictionaries and thesauruses.

Scanning

Scanning involves moving the eyes quickly down the page seeking specific words, phrases and ideas.

Here, we know what we are searching for, so can concentrate on finding a particular answer. Scanning is also used when we first find a resource to determine whether it will answer our questions.

It is also useful to scan parts of texts to see if they're going to be useful, for example:

* the introduction or abstract (if you are looking at a research paper)
* the first or last paragraphs of chapters
* the concluding chapter of a book or the conclusion of a research paper.

However, both skimming **and** scanning skills can be tricky for neurodivergent students, particularly those who have dyslexia in their profiles, as they require quick processing of visual-verbal information. This is an obstacle for those who have difficulty with word recognition or with visual processing/visual stress.

However, we have to use skimming and scanning, otherwise reading takes us too long to 'sift' out useful information. Here are some ideas which can help with skimming and scanning skills.

Skimming and scanning strategies

Create a personal glossary

Some students find that unfamiliar words cause them to stumble when reading. That is because these will not have been previously imprinted into their memory. It can take time to process new words and for our brains to connect meaning to them. One way of increasing your familiarity with new vocabulary is to create a personal glossary of subject-specific words.

> *A glossary is an alphabetical list of subject-related words with explanations or definitions.*

There are different ways of making your glossary. You might:

* buy an indexed book
* create an alphabetical list, digitally
* use index cards (either digital or physical).

At the minimum, every time you encounter a new word you should write it into your glossary and give a definition of the meaning.

 Use an internet search engine, built-in thesaurus/dictionaries in common software, or your smart speaker/phone assistant to give you definitions and synonyms for new words. Try asking 'Define the word sesquipedalian' and see what it says!

Depending on your subject and how your own memory works, you might need a little bit more than just a straightforward list of words and definitions. In this case, you could add some of the following details to your glossary:

* **Context:** Put the word into a sentence so you understand its usage.

* **Spelling reminder:** This works well if you need to remember specific words for exams. The idea of 'attaching' an unusual mental image to a word can work particularly well.

* **Base:** This is where you find out the root, or base, of the word (also known as etymology). If you understand where the word originated it can help you to unpick the reason for the spelling. This is often very helpful for dyslexic students when the written word simply does not match the spoken pronunciation or is very unfamiliar.

Here's an example from a trainee teacher's glossary (which uses index cards):

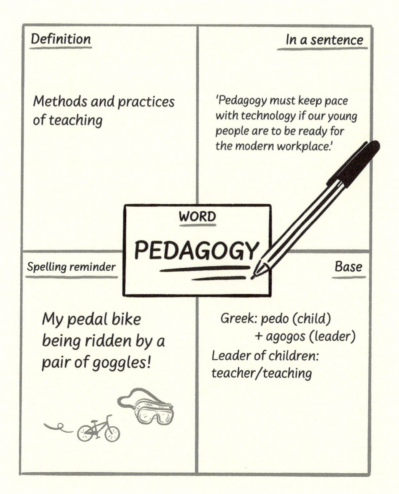

Here is a blank version of this for you to try.

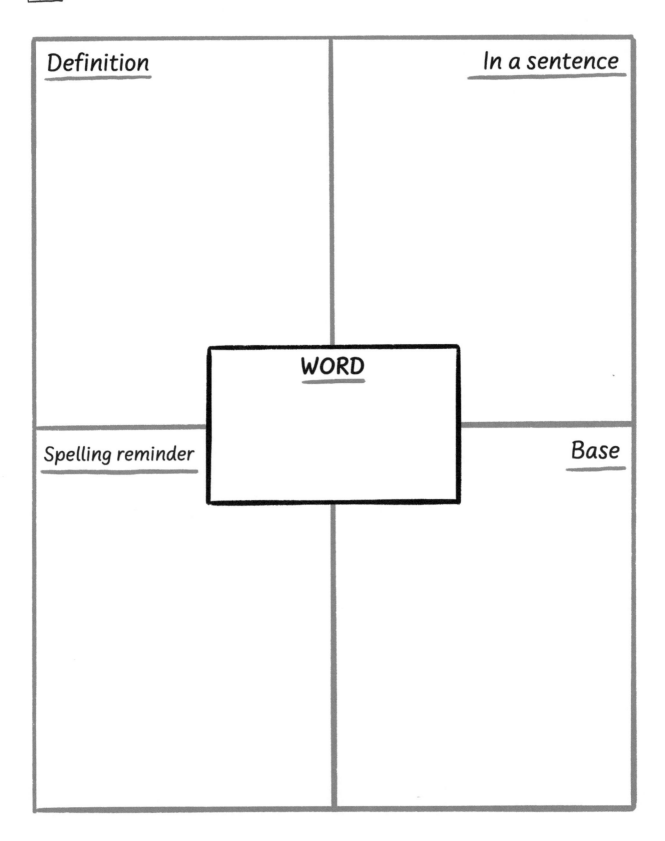

If you like drawing, you could add a sketch to your glossary to help embed this into your memory (for the word 'pedagogy' it might be a sketch of a pair of goggles riding a bike).

Using organizational features of text

'Organizational features' are the methods writers use to break up their work so that it is easier to find information.

An example of an organizational feature is the speech bubble above! Authors use these features to draw you to main ideas or key points and this is why it is useful to be able to take note of them. You can use them to help you to make sense of information.

When you are reading watch out for:

* headings and subheadings
* bold or italicized text
* sidebars or text boxes
* diagrams or images.

Looking at the 'shape' of a text

You might also like to think about the 'shape' of a text to help you understand how it is structured. Often different genres of writing have different conventions for the shape of their writing.

In many cultures, story-telling looks a bit like an arc.

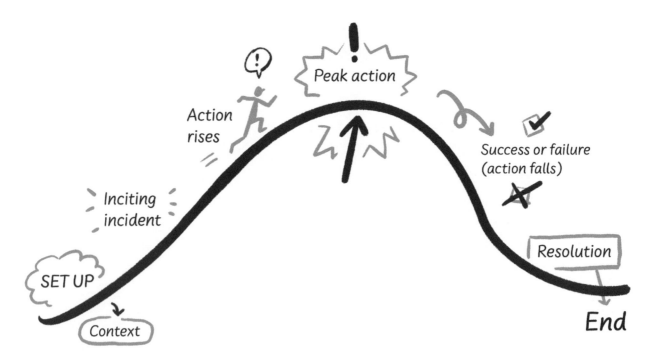

This is the same whether we are writing or telling a story. We usually start by setting the scene, describing what led up to an incident, talking about the aftermath and describing the conclusion to the story.

I think academic writing is also a bit like telling a story, and there's more about this in the section on structuring writing a bit later on. It's worth keeping the 'shape' of the text in your mind when you are trying to understand how it works, particularly if you tend towards being creative.

For example, if a text starts with a general point and then becomes more specific, you could think of it as being like an upside-down triangle. Many academic writers use this shape for their opening paragraphs and it's something you will probably be familiar with.

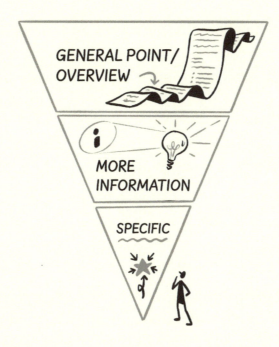

The impact of visual stress

> *Visual stress* can cause problems when reading, such as movement/blurring of text, glare, eye strain and headaches.

Using overlays, reading rulers or reading windows

Many neurodivergent students have some form of visual stress (sometimes known as Meares-Irlen syndrome). This can make reading physically uncomfortable. Coloured overlays, rulers or spectacles are often recommended to ease this problem.

However, research doesn't support the view that reading proficiency is improved when they are used.[1] This is controversial (and a bit confusing) because students often say that overlays really **do** help them. My personal view is that the colour is most likely reducing glare and if something is making reading less stressful for someone, then I can't see an issue. That said, I wouldn't advise spending huge amounts of money on specialist glasses unless you are absolutely certain they work for you.

If visual stress is causing you significant difficulties there are specialist opticians in most large towns; these are usually known as behavioural optometrists. They will be able to give you individual advice and guidance.

This is something any parents/carers might like to bear in mind. I have supported many children and young people prescribed with expensive, colour-tinted glasses. None wore them in school, though they told their grown-ups at home otherwise! They badly didn't want to appear 'different' and were much more likely to use coloured overlays or rulers.

Here are some self-help strategies that you can try to reduce visual stress.

Strategies to reduce visual stress

Off-white or cream paper

Ask for any work or handouts to be printed on off-white or cream paper. In my experience, this is often enough to reduce glare and make reading more comfortable. Keep in mind that if your visual stress is combined with dyslexia you will probably need additional adjustments to make reading more comfortable, such as accessible/dyslexia-friendly font styles and sizes, and double spacing.

Enlarged paper

Ask for enlarged paper. Certain types of paper, particularly graph paper, can be horrible to look at when there are so many lines close together. This problem can be reduced if the paper is bigger.

Use an overlay

These are clear pieces of coloured plastic which you can lay on top of the text you wish to read. They are widely available quite cheaply if you avoid specialist opticians and use the internet to source them. The quality will not be quite as good as from an optician, but they are a great starting point until you are sure they work. They are usually A4 and are easily scratched or bent so keep a few spare. You can cut them into smaller sections if you like.

Reading rulers

You can use a reading ruler which can easily be found online. These are smaller transparent overlays, usually roughly half the length of a standard ruler. They have a line printed horizontally, which is handy for following the lines of text. They come in a variety of different colours, which is helpful if you experience glare from white paper. They are also sturdier than A4 overlays so easier to carry around without damaging them. Their smaller size makes them more comfortable to use on pages that are smaller than A4, like most books. They fit into inside jacket pockets too, which is handy if you need to wear a jacket or blazer!

Reading windows

Use a reading window if you find a whole page of text (or figures) overwhelming. These are available to buy or you can easily make your own. These physically reduce the amount of text you can see.

> ### How to make a reading window
>
> You need an empty cereal box and scissors.
>
> To make:
>
> 1. Cut the cereal box into a rectangle to fit the size of the page you would like to read.
>
> 2. Cut a horizontal slit into the cardboard, so that you have a 'window' through which you can see the text. The size of this is up to you. You can make the window as small as one or two lines deep, or much larger.
>
> 3. Put your reading window shiny, printed-side down on the page.
>
> 4. Slide the reading window down the page as you read. It will look something like this:
>
>

So, we've looked at the different reading skills that are important for studying and have collected any physical materials which can make reading easier. The next step is finding or deciding what to read. Although reading can be prescribed to you, it is also important to use your critical thinking skills to find your own.

Finding and selecting source material

Before you start to read anything, you need to decide **what** you should be reading. Selecting relevant source material is a skill and this becomes increasingly challenging as you move towards higher-level studies.

Sometimes the source material will be provided for you. By the time you are working at the college or university level, you will almost certainly be using internet searches and library services to find your own source materials. These provide the evidence to back up your argument or main claims.

Well-chosen sources help you to show that:

* you understand the material
* you can apply your learning to the question
* you can explain the relevance of your ideas.

 *Read your essay question **and** any guidance notes extremely carefully. These usually list the source material you need or will direct you to certain sections/weeks where you can find it yourself.*

The quality of your source information matters. University and college libraries are reliable places to try first and they will be able to help you to make your searches more productive. Do not be afraid to ask for help as, in my experience, library staff genuinely enjoy supporting students. There are many reputable online research databases, and one popular search engine for finding academic sources is Google Scholar.

Researching online

The main thing to remember here is to be as specific as you can so that you are narrowing down your possible list of useful sources to begin with. Otherwise, it can take an age to work your way through the results trying to filter out irrelevant information.

How to approach an online search:

* Start by writing down the main ideas that you are trying to research. What are the key terms?

* Decide if there are any synonyms or alternative definitions that are used in the topic you are investigating.

> A **synonym** is a word that means the same or almost the same in any sentence. A synonym for 'search' might be 'investigation'.

Example: using search terms

I might be interested in reading some research about dyspraxia. It would be useful for me to know that dyspraxia is also known as Developmental Coordination Disorder (DCD), so I could widen my search words and ensure that I do not miss important reading.

You need to choose your search terms carefully and some methods can help with this:

* Be specific if you can. You may already know the author of the work you are looking for; if so, be sure to include that in your search term.

* If you are very specific about what you want to look for, put your whole search phrase into speech marks. Then the search will only find sources that include this phrase.

* You can use an asterisk at the end of a word to show that there might be a range of different word endings, so the word 'child*' will also pick up research which has 'children' or 'childlike' in the title.

* You can use the word 'or' to link your search terms when they might share similar meanings. Perhaps I am writing an essay about the impact of the Covid-19 pandemic on younger people. I might use the phrase 'impact of Covid-19 on adolescents or young people'.

* You can use 'and' to find results which link the ideas you are trying to research. I could use 'impact of Covid-19 and teenagers'.

* You can use 'not' to exclude terms that will clutter your research. So, you could say 'not adults' if you were not interested in the impact of the pandemic on adults.

Keep a record of your searches and the search terms you have used. This will save lots of repeated effort if you have to come back and find additional information later, and your tutors may want you to list your search terms in your work too.

Once you have found some potential sources you need to be able to read and understand them, which is what we will look at in the next section.

Reading and understanding source material strategies

Strategies that help you read and understand your source material often take some time to get the hang of and so you will need to give yourself a chance to get used to them. Initially, it might actually make reading slower for you! This is one of those irritating situations where practice really does make perfect, so keep at it and refer to the quick self-care tips in Chapter 2 if you need to. There are several reading strategies available, but I have chosen the three that most of my students like to use, namely:

* **KWL** (know, want-to-know, learned)
* **What, how, why?**
* **SQ3R** (survey, question, read, recite, review).

Each of these works on the basis that you are proactively engaging with the writing rather than trying to passively retain information. You can try them all and see which one (or ones) works best for you. Remember too that if you have enjoyed using the Cornell note-taking method (covered in Chapter 5), you could also try that for making notes from readings.

KWL (know, want-to-know, learned)

KWL was first introduced by Professor Donna Ogle[2] in the 1980s as a tool for understanding non-fiction. It is a method that is excellent when you are reading with a straightforward purpose in mind; for example, perhaps you are trying to find particular information for an assignment. It uses a table.

Know	Want-to-know	Learned
Write what you already know about the issue.	Create questions to interrogate the text so that you can find out what you want to know.	Write what you have learned from this text. Did it answer your question? Do you need to find more from elsewhere? What is that?

Here is an example from a student who is undertaking research for an essay discussing the difference between equality and equity.

Know	Want-to-know	Learned
Equality and equity don't mean the same things, but people get confused (including me).	What is the definition and difference between equality and equity?	Equality is defined in this text as 'treating everybody exactly the same, regardless of personal characteristics; providing the same to all'. Equity is defined in this text as 'recognizing that not everyone starts from an equal position; allocating resources and making adjustments to account for this'. I still need to know more about the history and origins of these terms for my intro.

This is particularly useful as a prompt to look for other sources.

 Here is a blank KWL table for you to use.

Know	Want-to-know	Learned
What I already know	*What questions do I need to answer?*	*What I found out and what I still need to know*

What, how, why?

This method might work well for you if you are studying a subject which relies more on subjective views and inference, perhaps a creative writing or literature course. That's because it asks you to think about the methods and devices the writer has used and asks you to consider how the information is being communicated rather than just the facts that are included. It works well if you have a copy of the text that you can make notes on (either digitally or by hand).

You need to answer these three questions as you read through (so think about the different sections of the text as well as the overall text):

1. What does it tell me?

2. How does it tell me?

3. Why does it tell me?

Let's look at an example.

> ### Extract from *The Adventure of the Engineer's Thumb* by Sir Arthur Conan-Doyle[3]
>
> Sherlock Holmes was, as I expected, lounging about his sitting-room in his dressing-gown, reading the agony column of *The Times* and smoking his before-breakfast pipe, which was composed of all the plugs and dottles left from his smokes of the day before, all carefully dried and collected on the corner of the mantelpiece. He received us in his quietly genial fashion, ordered fresh rashers and eggs, and joined us in a hearty meal. When it was concluded he settled our new acquaintance upon the sofa, placed a pillow beneath his head, and laid a glass of brandy and water within his reach.

Reading and Understanding Source Material

What does it tell me?	How does it tell me?	Why does it tell me?
Describes what happens when Watson and the engineer arrive at Baker Street. Describes breakfast scene.	Lounging (verb – idea of relaxed attitude). Casually (adverb) smoking. Aided by phrases like 'quietly genial' and 'reading the agony column'. Breakfast is 'hearty' and he orders food after they have arrived. Before-breakfast pipe (alliteration) – idea of comfort/habits – 'as I expected'.	Points to Sherlock's character and attitude on the day in question. Likes comfort, relaxed starts, routines/rituals (breakfast, smoking). Does these things first before he settles the engineer. Suggests he may not like/do interruptions to his routines. Creature of habit? Remains entirely cool and collected. Unruffled despite arrival of injured man.

Here is a template you could use if you would like to try this way of reading.

What does it tell me?	How does it tell me?	Why does it tell me?

SQ3R (survey, question, read, recite, review)

This method was introduced by Professor Frances Robinson in 1941.[4] It is well established and recommended by many colleges and universities today. This is an excellent strategy for reading that is more complex, where you are looking to identify themes and concepts rather than just finding straightforward information.

The questioning element here is very important. It means you are reading **for a purpose** from the start. You will be thinking about your questions as you read. That means you are more likely to be able to make connections and notice key information.

Reciting (saying it aloud) and reviewing the information means that you are more likely to retain the information you have read. This is shown to help comprehension.[5]

Do not be put off by the number of steps in the process. Once you are familiar with it, it can become like second nature and can really help you to approach a text critically.

Reading and Understanding Source Material

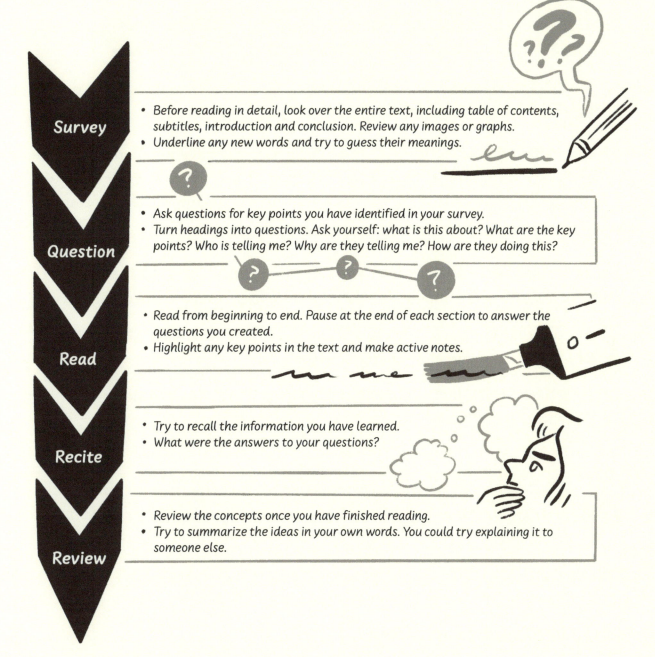

 To search for a particular word in a pdf document use these commands:

Ctrl + F (for Windows)

Cmd + F (for Mac)

Then put the word you are looking for in the search box.

Using technology to help with reading skills

In-built accessibility features

Most common operating systems and web browsers now have excellent, ready-to-go accessibility features. I encourage you to explore these and see if any are useful for you. With my usual caveat about the rapidly changing nature of these features, I would recommend you try these:

* Read-aloud functions – Microsoft and Google products have this feature in their word-processing functions. Your computer can read the document to you.

* Immersive reader – most web browsers have immersive screen readers which will read text to you in a very natural voice.

* Microsoft Windows Narrator functionality (press the Windows logo key with the Control key and hit Enter).

Software companies produce great online tutorials for their accessibility features. Just type 'accessibility features' and the name of your system into an internet search engine. These will also be kept up to date!

Tech to help with visual stress

There is also a range of different options for virtual coloured overlays and reading rulers (some free, some paid-for). These provide a wide variety of different 'tints' for your screen and it is well worth investigating if these make reading feel less visually stressful for you.

Equally, screen magnifier apps can be very helpful.

Using AI

You could also consider asking an AI bot to summarize a text for you, to make this easier for you to read and to give you a sense of its contents. I would urge some caution with this as they do not always accurately represent the information, which can change the meaning. Again, please **do not** use AI if your institution prohibits it.

This chapter has concentrated on finding all of the materials you need to write and on being able to read and understand them. The next step is to be able to pull all of this information together into a cohesive piece of writing – not easy! That's what we will look at in detail, in the next chapter.

 Let's recap

In this chapter we have covered:

- skimming and scanning
- creating a personal glossary
- using organizational features of text
- visual stress and strategies to help
- finding and selecting source materials
- researching online
- reading and understanding source material
- three reading strategies
- using tech to help
- using AI.

> **Key takeaway messages from this chapter**
>
> - Reading is hard and needs to be 'active' for information to stick in your brain.
> - It's worth taking some time to find a reading strategy that works for you.
> - Use technology to help if you can.
> - Librarians are great for supporting you with research skills.

Chapter 7

COMPLETING ASSIGNMENTS, ESSAYS AND DISSERTATIONS

Pulling lots of different information together to create a clear, well-evidenced and well-organized piece of writing is not a straightforward task.

Writing as a process

The most important thing to understand at the outset is that writing is a process and that it's crucial to complete every part of this cycle to achieve your best marks. This section will walk you through each of these stages in detail, breaking them down into steps and giving you different strategies to try out.

Stage one: using feedback

This might feel like it should come at the end of the process, but actually, it's the first thing you should check (unless of course, this is your first piece of work). Most teachers and lecturers work hard to ensure that marking is accurate and constructive. It seems a shame not to use it to help improve your learning.

That said, taking feedback on board is not always easy and might even feel a little confronting. This is particularly the case if you have worked very hard and your grade is not what you hoped for. However, reading and acting on feedback helps you to:

* identify your strengths and build on these
* find out areas that you need to work on and develop
* improve your subject knowledge
* prepare for your next assignment to improve your marks.

To digest and reflect on feedback you can:

* review the essay marking criteria to find any knowledge 'gaps' you can fill
* talk through your feedback with a peer
* ask your teacher or lecturer to explain anything you don't understand
* write a list of points to remember for your next assignment.

 *When reflecting on your learning look for **patterns** in your performance. Are you getting consistently great feedback in some areas and not-so-great in others? Pattern recognition is often a neurodivergent strength, particularly if you are autistic. You can play to that by jotting down anything you have noticed and going back through other assignments to help identify any patterns. This helps you to work out where you should be targeting your greatest efforts.*

Completing Assignments, Essays and Dissertations

You can also use a reflective model to frame your ideas. This works well if you are finding that marking feels very personal as it helps to give some objective structure to your thinking.

Kolb's experiential cycle[1] is a popular one with my students, and with lecturers/tutors.

Here's an example:

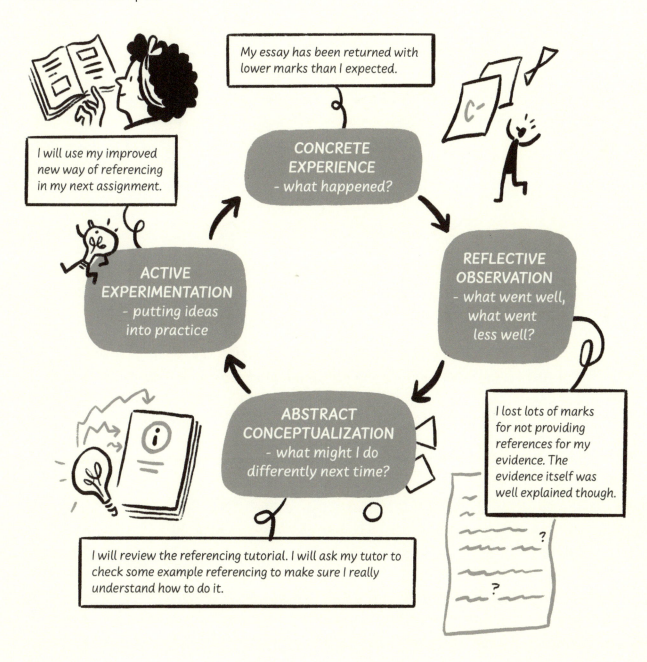

143

Here's a template loosely based on this cycle for you to plan your reflections.

 If you are struggling to motivate yourself to write, try looking through some previous work where you obtained good feedback. This helps remind yourself about your good writing skills and can also boost your self-esteem.

Stage two: understanding the question

Now you have your feedback in mind, you can move on to look at the question. The first and most important thing is to ensure that you fully understand it. This is not always easy, particularly when you are working at university or college level when questions often come with pages of guidance. Remember that it is fine to check your understanding with your tutor if you're not sure!

Let's take this as our sample exercise for this section:

'Discuss the impact of the war between the USSR and Afghanistan on the members of the Warsaw Pact and consider how this influenced the outcome of the Cold War.'

There are a few steps you can take to ensure that you fully understand the exercise and don't miss anything important:

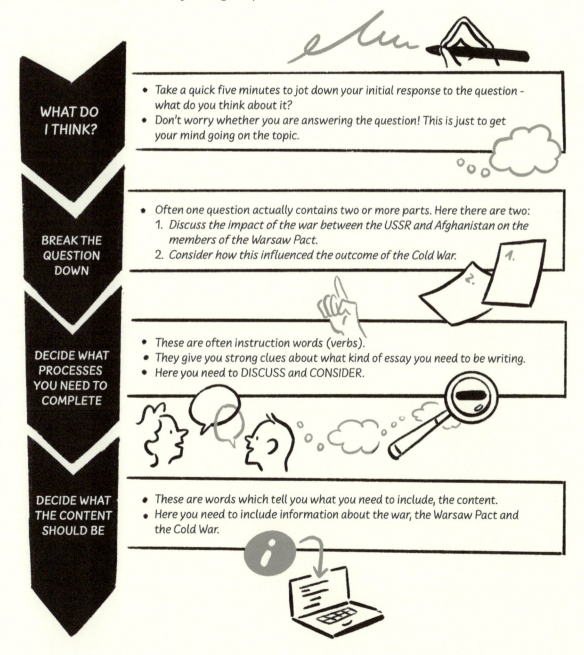

WHAT DO I THINK?
- Take a quick five minutes to jot down your initial response to the question - what do you think about it?
- Don't worry whether you are answering the question! This is just to get your mind going on the topic.

BREAK THE QUESTION DOWN
- Often one question actually contains two or more parts. Here there are two:
  1. *Discuss the impact of the war between the USSR and Afghanistan on the members of the Warsaw Pact.*
  2. *Consider how this influenced the outcome of the Cold War.*

DECIDE WHAT PROCESSES YOU NEED TO COMPLETE
- These are often instruction words (verbs).
- They give you strong clues about what kind of essay you need to be writing.
- Here you need to DISCUSS and CONSIDER.

DECIDE WHAT THE CONTENT SHOULD BE
- These are words which tell you what you need to include, the content.
- Here you need to include information about the war, the Warsaw Pact and the Cold War.

> *If you are still stuck, try rewriting the question in your own words. Use synonyms (words which have the same meaning within a sentence).*

Example: a student has rewritten a question in their own words

English is the world's lingua franca. To what extent is this desirable?

Becomes:

English is the most universally understood language in the world. How beneficial is this? Remember to say why!

You can also see the student has written a little note to themselves at the end of the rewritten question to make sure they remember to give lots of reasons for their ideas.

Processing or instruction words

There are many different kinds of processing or instruction words (which are usually verbs telling you what action you need to take). Have a look at the table on the next page for some examples.

Key process	Process you need to complete
Evaluate or critically evaluate	Consider the pros and cons of something and then explain to what extent this is useful or effective. You need to make a judgement about the issue you are writing about. You should have an argument which runs through this kind of question.
Discuss	A discussion is a conversation, so think of this as giving different points of view on a subject. You would usually explain which of these views seems the strongest or has the most supporting evidence.
Explain	This is more descriptive. You need to make sure that you describe something clearly.
Analyse	Here you need to look at the issue in depth, looking at it from different perspectives and trying to work out how these ideas link together. You might be able to identify different themes in this kind of question.
Compare and contrast	You are describing at least two different areas/issues and saying what is similar and different about them.
Examine	Look at your issue very closely, noting anything that agrees with your existing understanding or challenges it.
Explore	This is an extension of the idea of examining a subject. Here you will look at your issue more broadly. Think about whether there is anything particularly debatable about it. Think about the context in which it 'sits'.
Illustrate	Use examples to help explain or describe the issue you are discussing. This could be written examples or you might use images, diagrams, graphs or tables.
Summarize	Pull together the key issues and ideas around your topic and outline them clearly and concisely.

 Keep the question and the assignment guidance open on your screen all the time that you are writing up your work. Tick off each section as you complete it. That helps to ensure that you haven't missed anything!

Selecting what information or content to include

As your studies progress, you will be asked to make more decisions about the information you wish to include and this will be selected from a much wider range of source material.

This is something that students often find difficult. It can be tempting to include too much information, for fear of missing anything important. This can make your points feel muddled and uncertain.

So, when you are deciding what to include in your writing always keep in mind:

* **What** point are you trying to get across?
* **How** is this relevant to the question?
* **Why should your reader be interested in your point?**

 *This last point is very important. You might imagine you have a rude goblin sitting behind you as you are writing, yelling at you 'Yeah, but why should I care?' If you can't explain **why**, then your information is likely to be irrelevant or poorly explained.*

You can take the following steps to ensure that your content is appropriate:

1. Look through your class notes.

2. Recap any other sources you have been pointed to which relate to these topics.

3. Select those which are most relevant (this is the difficult bit).

4. Highlight any key evidence you would like to use (such as useful quotes and ideas).

Completing Assignments, Essays and Dissertations

If you are worrying that you haven't included correct or relevant information you can try putting your sources into a table like this.

What I've included	Where I found it	How/why it relates to the question

 Here is a downloadable copy of this table.

 Remember to avoid confirmation bias when selecting sources. You usually need to consider alternative viewpoints — to compare, contrast or argue. These might not always agree with your own ideas! Question your thinking: 'Does everyone feel like this?' They almost certainly don't.

Confirmation bias is when we look for sources or information which support our view, as well as interpreting and analysing information in a way that tends to agree with our pre-existing ideas.

Stage three: making a plan

We have already established that writing is a process and that the first part of this is ensuring that you fully understand the question. The next step is planning for writing which is broken down into three steps in this section:

1. Decide the purpose, audience, format and tone of your writing.

2. Decide the structure you would like to use.

3. Write a plan.

If you plan **really** well, drafting your actual essay should be a piece of cake. However, as I know from working with so many students over the years, many skip the planning stage altogether. Please hear me out as I try to explain why it is absolutely vital.

Why bother planning?

> *I know what I want to say. Planning just wastes time!*

Students often say this to me. For a very basic piece of writing, it might just about hold true. However, the further you progress through your academic career, the more important planning becomes.

That's because examiners are checking that you can pull together ideas from multiple sources and evaluate your findings. This means you must **show** how clever you are at gathering information, sorting, analysing this and putting it all into one coherent piece of writing. It's a bit like waving a flag and shouting 'Look how much I know!'

Completing Assignments, Essays and Dissertations

It is very difficult to maintain coherence if you haven't planned as there's just too much information to mentally sort on the fly as you write. You also run the risk of missing important themes or linking points, and it is this kind of evaluation which helps you to gain higher marks. When I am marking my own students' work, I can always tell who has planned and who has not because of this last point.

> *I'm only in my first year at uni or still at school, so I don't need to plan yet!*

The early years are exactly when you should be developing excellent planning skills as the stakes are not too high. I promise that you will look back and be glad you did!

Step one of planning

Before you start to plan, ask yourself four important questions:

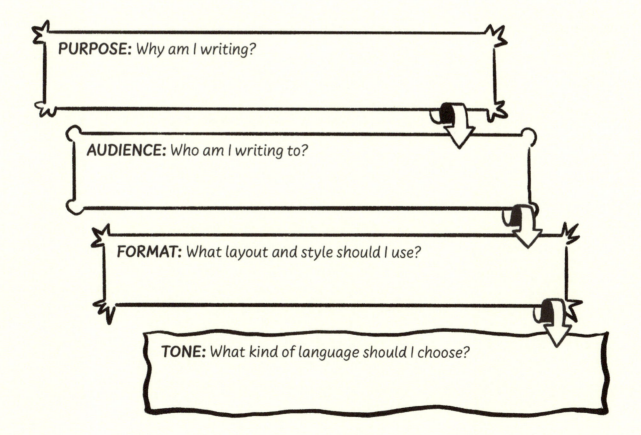

PURPOSE: Why am I writing?

AUDIENCE: Who am I writing to?

FORMAT: What layout and style should I use?

TONE: What kind of language should I choose?

The answer to these questions will help you to write in a way that is appropriate for the context. These will usually depend on what is conventional for the kind of writing you are undertaking.

Let's break these questions down a bit more:

The purpose: why are you writing?

The answer can be quite complicated because we are usually writing for a mixture of reasons.

Of course, you are writing because you would like to get good marks and a decent qualification in the end! However, when you are planning, you really need to focus on the purpose of the brief rather than your personal goals (though following the brief should lead to good grades).

Broadly, there are four main types of purposes of text. Have a look at the examples and you will see that each purpose has a different kind of writing style.

Text type to:	Purpose	Example
Instruct	To tell you how to do something	Booklets that come with new products: 'Rinse this kettle with clean water before use.' Short sentences with commanding verbs
Persuade	To try and get you to do something	Advertisements: 'This is the best kettle you will ever boil!' Exaggerated language and catchy phrasing
Inform (Explain)	To give you explanatory information about something	Non-fiction textbooks, information signage: 'Kettles are often made of stainless steel as this is a hygienic surface for cleaning purposes.' Factual, formal language, with main facts often backed up with further information and evidence
Describe	To try to paint a visual picture of something	Fiction writing, generally anything that tries to set the scene: 'The kettle's stainless steel shell shone in the bright sunshine.' Use of descriptive language features (here it's repeated 's' sounds)

Most of us need to switch between these different types of writing styles depending on the task. Students often spend most of their time writing to inform (explain).

The audience: who are you writing to?

Pay close attention to the audience too, as this is something that students can forget. It will change your writing style. You wouldn't write the same way to your friends as you would to your tutor!

Depending on your course, you may be writing for more than one audience and this can be tricky.

> Here's an example from a law course:
>
> **Question:** Prepare a discussion brief for senior partners in your organization, describing the implications of recent changes concerning health and safety at work legislation as these relate to retail workers. You should detail relevant case law and the impact this might have on the management of future client proposals.
>
> Here you are required to role-play as a more junior lawyer within a legal firm, producing a document to help more senior partners make decisions. That means you will probably use 'we' when you're writing, which is quite unusual. For example, in your conclusion, you might say 'We should consider the case implications of this carefully as neglecting to address these concerns may prove costly to us.'
>
> You also have the secondary audience of your teacher or lecturer to consider. That means following the referencing conventions of your school, college or university although a 'real' legal firm may use an entirely different system.

Format: what layout should I use (what should it look like)?

There are usually rules about how your educational institution likes things to look on the page. For example, most universities prefer work to be submitted in double-line spacing, and a font no smaller than 11 pt.

There are also typical conventions for different types of text. For example, a business letter will be laid out differently from an email.

 The exact style of layout will be different depending on where and what you are studying. So, it's best to check with your teachers.

Tone: what kind of language should I use?

Tone is mainly set by your word choice. It sets the 'mood' of our writing and affects how the reader feels. It's often related to conventions in writing. For example, 'I think these numbers are a bit dodgy' wouldn't sound right in an academic assignment. 'The validity of this data is questionable' feels much more appropriate, as it's more formal and objective.

You can find out more about academic writing style towards the end of this chapter.

Example: changing format and tone according to purpose

Two students are completing their assignments.

A business studies student is analysing data from a case study and writing a report with recommendations. Their language is factual and objective. They will include tables and graphs with statistics to support their findings. They will structure their work using subheadings and the recommendations will be formatted using bullet points.

Completing Assignments, Essays and Dissertations

> An English literature student is comparing themes across three poetry pieces. They will describe various literary features using several language devices. They will write an essay which uses continuous text and paragraphs without subheadings.

Once you are sure that you have fully understood the context and the audience you can start to think about an appropriate structure for your work.

Step two of planning: deciding on the structure of your writing

The importance of having a cohesive structure in your writing cannot be overemphasized. I like to think of my students as taking their audience on a journey through their writing. You can think of it as being like a walk through a forest. The student needs to be the leader and if they aren't clear about their own direction, the following audience will get lost!

You can avoid this by deciding upon a structure which suits your purpose and by making this **explicitly clear** throughout by using signposting words and phrases (these are explained in the next chapter).

So, every assignment needs a clear beginning, middle and end. This is the classic three-part structure:

1. introduction

2. main body

3. conclusion.

The beginning – structure of an introduction

The point of your introduction is to set the scene for your audience so they know what they are going to be reading about and why. You need to make sure they understand what to expect.

A typical structure for an introduction is to go from making more general points to being more specific. You can think of this as being a bit like an upside-down triangle. The question being considered here is: Compare and contrast religious symbolism used in Shakespeare's Julius Caesar and *Hamlet*.

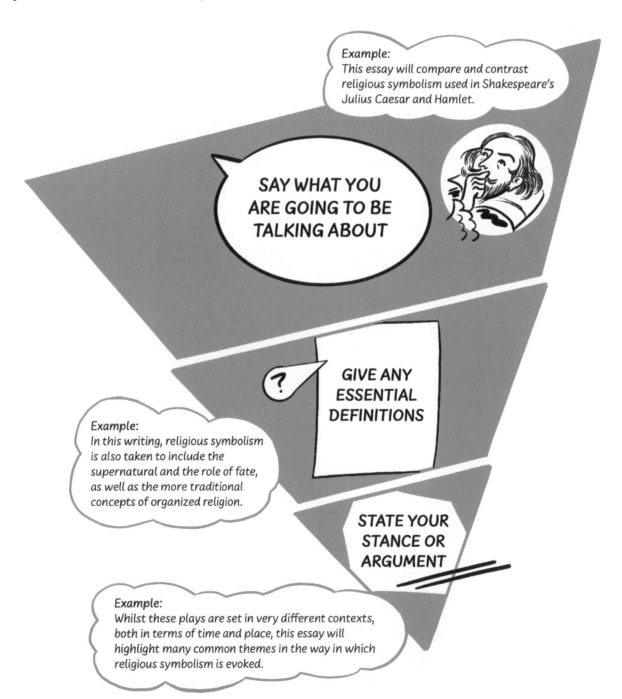

The ending – structure of a conclusion

Something very important here is not to include any new information! This section should draw together your main points, summarizing your rationale and explaining how the content supports your central stance or argument. It's also your final chance to remind the audience what you have been discussing, so remember to refer back to the original question too.

Students often feel like they are repeating themselves here, so remember to use your paraphrasing skills (look at the section called 'Writing succinctly: summarizing and paraphrasing' a bit later in this chapter). This helps you to vary the way you are discussing the previous information you've given, without changing the meaning.

> ## Example conclusion
>
> This assignment has provided an in-depth comparison of the role of religious symbolism in *Julius Caesar* and *Hamlet*. It has explored the contrasts in how this has been employed by Shakespeare. It concludes that, despite the entirely different contexts for the plays, there is an overwhelming number of similarities between how religious symbolism is used within the chosen texts.

The structure of introductions and conclusions in assignments largely stays the same. However, deciding on the structure of your main content can be trickier and so that's what we'll look at next.

Deciding the structure for your main body

This decision will very much depend on the type of question you are answering and the level of your studies. Some of the most common structures for an essay are described below.

Chronological or cause-and-effect

This is the most straightforward structure. It works well for essays which are most descriptive or explanatory. Here you are making your points in the order of events.

For example, you may be writing about a historical battle. You begin by outlining the context of the battle, then you describe each stage of the battle (in date order), and finally, you describe the impact of the battle upon the wider context (the extent to which it influenced the outcome of the war).

Compare and contrast structure

These are useful for giving different viewpoints and are very common in academic writing. There are two different ways of doing these kinds of essays. You can either group your ideas in blocks, or you can link them thematically.

* Blocking means taking each part of the question in turn and discussing the ideas more linearly.

* Using a thematic structure involves grouping the ideas which relate to the question.

Let's look at an example so you can see what I mean.

Two ways of structuring a 'compare and contrast' question

Question: Compare and contrast religious symbolism used in Shakespeare's *Julius Caesar* and *Hamlet*.

Blocked plan	Thematic plan
Introduction • brief outline of the plot for both plays • define religious symbolism • state argument: similar usage despite different settings. Religious symbolism in *Hamlet* • ghost of Hamlet's father • references to Christianity/the Bible • role of fate and divine intervention. Religious symbolism in *Julius Caesar* • omens and supernatural events • reference to ancient Roman religion • role of destiny and the gods. Comparison of religious symbolism in *Hamlet* and *Julius Caesar* • similarities in the use of religious symbolism • differences in the portrayal of religion • how the use of religious symbolism contributes to the themes of the plays. Conclusion • recap key points • return to central argument • highlight importance of religious symbolism in Shakespeare's plays • final thoughts and implications for understanding the plays.	Introduction • brief outline of plot for both plays • define religious symbolism • state argument: similar usage despite different settings. Theme 1: fate and destiny • overview of theme • how this is portrayed in both plays • highlight similarities and differences. Theme 2: role of organized or institutional religion • overview of theme • how this is portrayed in both plays • highlight similarities and differences. Theme 3: the supernatural • overview of theme • how this is portrayed in both plays • highlight similarities and differences. Conclusion • recap key points • return to central argument • highlight importance of religious symbolism in Shakespeare's plays • final thoughts and implications for understanding the plays.

There are advantages and disadvantages to each of these approaches, which are summarized in the following table.

Style	Advantages	Disadvantages
Blocked	• straightforward and easy to plan • easy for readers to see the progression of ideas.	• can lead to repetition as you have to refer back to each of the areas you have already described when you are doing your analysis • difficult to demonstrate deeper understanding of how ideas are interrelated across different sources • can become very unwieldy if you are comparing more than two texts or sources.
Thematic	• enables you to show a deeper understanding of interrelated ideas • minimal repetition risk.	• needs careful planning so that linked ideas aren't missed • can feel more complicated to write • needs lots more signposting so the audience understands the progression of ideas, e.g., phrases like, 'having considered X, it is important to discuss Y'.

Problem and solution structures

These are also very common in academic writing. Here you must consider an issue (the problem) and discuss possible ways of resolving these (the solution). The problem might be practical or theoretical and this will depend on the subject you are studying.

You will be required to analyse the situation carefully and usually say which solution seems the best to you (justifying your reasons).

> ## An example problem and solution question
>
> Young drivers are at greater risk of having accidents compared to those over 25. Consider the reasons for this and explore ways to mitigate these.
>
> A typical structure for this kind of assignment could look like this:

1. Introduction: State the problem under discussion, explain any key terms/definitions and state your argument. Signpost contents (tell the audience your structure).

2. Main body: Describe the problem in detail, and give evidence for the extent and impact of the problem. Place the problem in its wider context and consider broader implications.

3. Give a range of different solutions, using evidence. Explain the impact of these solutions – advantages and disadvantages. Compare and contrast these as you write, using words such as 'whereas', 'in contrast', 'alternatively' etc.

4. Conclusion: Restate the problem. Pull together the evidence you have already stated and show how this supports your opening argument (remember, there should be no new information in your conclusion).

Reflective writing structure

It seems that students are being asked to write reflective assignments more regularly. Often these require you to use a model upon which to base your reflection. One that seems to be used a lot is Kolb's reflective cycle,[2] which was discussed in my previous section about using feedback to improve your writing. Here's a reminder:

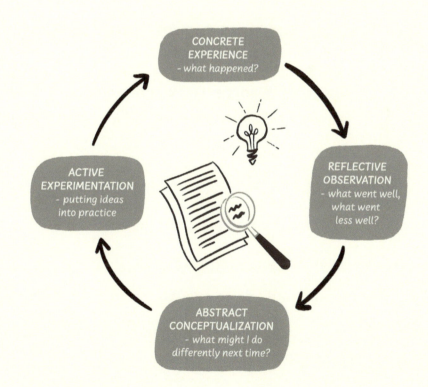

Just like any other assignment, your reflective piece should have a clear introduction, main body and conclusion. If you have been asked to use a reflective model, you must ensure that you explicitly refer to this, both in your introduction and in your main body. For example, you could state: 'I will be using Kolb's reflective cycle (1984) to frame my reflection.' Note that I have included an in-text citation and would put the full reference at the end. Reflective pieces should still be accurately referenced. This is because your writing should be personal but still academic in tone.

In the main body of your writing, you should continue to signpost any model or reflective framework you have been asked to use. You can use the first person in your reflection, so you might start a paragraph with something like: 'I will now move on to discuss the concrete steps I intend to take to improve. This is the action planning part of the model (Kolb, 1984).'

If you do not have a model upon which to base your reflection, it would still be sensible to use a kind of chronological structure.

Example structure for reflective writing

1. Introduction: What I will be looking at and why I have chosen this. Signpost the contents: 'I will be evaluating [whatever you have decided to evaluate] and then finishing with an action plan.'

2. What happened?

3. How did I think or feel when it was happening?

4. What do I think went well? Why?

5. What do I think went less well? Why?

6. What could I do to change this next time (my action plan)?

7. Conclusion: Summarize what you think you have learned from this experience.

There's a blank template you can use to plan this kind of reflection earlier in this chapter.

Step three of planning: making your plan – four popular planning techniques

By now, you will have the question clearly in mind, have gathered your sources and worked out what you think a good structure might be. That should allow you to make a great plan.

 When you plan, you can note down the sources for your evidence alongside each point. That way, when you write up you don't have to worry about hunting them down. It's also a good way of checking that you have some evidence for every point you are making!

Here are some planning methods that my students like to use.

Using bullet points or lists

This is probably the most common and familiar method. Here, you take key points from the assignment brief and transfer these into a series of bullet points, under which you can then add further bullet points listing the content you need to include.

Let's take my previous law exercise as an example:

'Prepare a discussion brief for senior partners in your organization, describing the implications of recent changes concerning health and safety at work legislation as these relate to retail workers. You should detail relevant case law and the impact this might have on the management of future client proposals.'

A bulleted plan might look something like this:

* introduction
* outline recent changes in law relating to health and safety in retail settings
* case law examples

* implications for the way the firm deals with client queries in this area
* conclusion.

You can then transfer these bullet headings directly into your assignment document and build it from there.

Advantages of bullet points/list	Disadvantages of bullet points/lists
Straightforward. Easy to see – neat and tidy. Very structured/linear. Acts like a checklist within your assignment so you can go back and ensure you have included everything.	Can't always see the big links between ideas and themes. Doesn't work well for people who don't think in linear ways. Might feel a bit constraining.

Using sticky note lists

This method is a little like an extension of using bullet points, but here you put the key points from the brief on to individual sticky notes to form a series of headings. You then use other sticky notes for the contents you need to use under each of those headings.

Advantages of sticky note lists	Disadvantages of sticky note lists
Good if you don't like making mistakes – you just move the note to change the order, so no rewriting. Works well for thematic structures. You can colour code your notes: one colour for main ideas/themes.	Can feel too messy and look confusing. Sticky notes can fall off walls or desks – always take a photo of your plan!

Using sticky note wheels

These are almost like simplified mind maps. You put your title on a sticky note in the middle and then have your ideas coming out from the centre like a series of spokes on a bicycle wheel on a series of individual sticky notes. Each spoke represents one main theme or idea in your essay.

Advantages of sticky note wheels	**Disadvantage of sticky note wheels**
Looks less messy than a standard mind map.	Space – unless you have a big wall this can cause issues.
Can help you to identify/link similar themes.	Sticky notes fall off – take a photo!
Easy to add to, take away and shift things around.	Some students find this too messy.
You can colour code your 'spokes'. You can have another code to show where ideas are linked or intersect.	

Using mind maps

I adore mind maps, but they are very much 'love it or hate it'. I know from my students that some find them visually confusing and messy, while others think they are the best thing since sliced bread. My dyslexic students generally love them, as do many with ADHD in their profiles. You can hand-draw mind maps or use software to help you.

Hand-drawn mind maps can look unstructured but often work well. I think they look a bit like jellyfish if you imagine them viewed from above!

To create a mind map do the following:

* Put your essay title or question in the centre.

* Create a series of tentacles radiating out from this, which are the main ideas under discussion.

* Expand upon your main ideas by adding secondary information on the fronds of these tentacles.

* Link some of your 'tentacles' together when you find that your themes are intersecting (think of how the tentacles of the jellyfish are often entwined).

* Consider using colour and images to help you differentiate between different ideas.

You will probably end up looking at something quite messy, but which is very effective (and I think beautiful) when looked at as a whole. Definitely a bit like a jellyfish.

Here is an example:

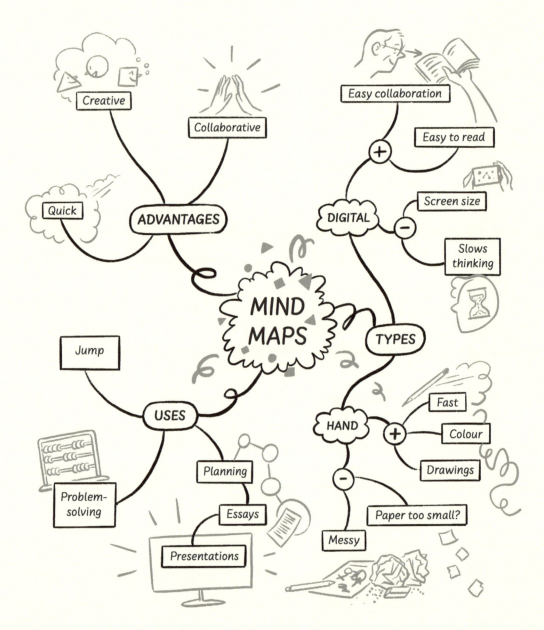

Mind-mapping technology

As I write, AI is just starting to be able to create mind maps. Users can input a chunk of text which is then summarized and made into a mind map for you. If your educational institution allows you to use AI like this, then it might seem like a fabulous thing!

However, you won't be surprised to hear me say that my views on this are mixed. It could certainly reduce the load on your working memory, but my experience is that many neurodivergent students develop their own unique mind-mapping style over time. That process of summarizing and linking information in a kind of 'bigger picture thinking' way is a good way of reinforcing knowledge. It also plays to the common neurodivergent strength of being able to visualize a problem in a broader context. It seems a shame to potentially stifle that by using AI.

However, there are some times when it might be helpful. If you would like to experiment with AI mind mapping then perhaps you could use it to help you 'translate' chunks of material into a more readable format for you. Do make sure that doesn't breach your institution's rules, though. I can see that this could work well for some students, particularly those with dyslexia in their profiles, as it removes all of those 'extra' words in English which don't carry much meaning (the little words like 'a' and 'the').

If you would like to use tech to create your own mind maps from scratch, then there are many apps available. I have tried out some of the free versions and have created a mini-review of each below. Please note that there are plenty of alternatives available and that these have been picked pretty randomly, just based on the fact that I know my students have tried them out. Tech is also changing at a rate of knots, so do check out the features for yourselves in case they have changed by the time you are reading this.

All of them are simple to sign up to and work in browsers as well as having apps, so you can use them anywhere.

Coggle

The screen opens with a tutorial which is really useful as you don't have to hunt around for a 'how to'. It has a clean look about it and there is more blank space on the screen compared to Canva or Miro. This makes it easy to focus on the ideas being worked on rather than on the features of Coggle itself. This might be useful if you are someone who is distracted by making things look pretty! There is a list of shortcuts on the screen which is helpful.

It is very easy to share mind maps with others and to work collaboratively in the app. This could be very useful for planning group projects and presentations.

Miro.com

This is very much designed for collaborative sessions for problem-solving in teams, so at first sight, it can seem more of a management tool than a student writing tool. It is easy to use, but it was not always immediately apparent where to go in the app to find help. There are plenty of YouTube tutorials to talk you through how to use it. This could also be very useful for group work.

Canva.com

Canva describes itself as a free whiteboard. There is a useful tour at the start and some good templates which you can start with. There is a dotted grid on the whiteboard which is useful for alignment and helpful if you like things to look neat and tidy. However, this might not be enjoyed by those with visual stress (I expect you can probably turn it off). It is very easy to share ideas with others.

Mind maps – a summary

Advantages of using mind maps	Disadvantages of using mind maps
• Speedy method of recording info if your mind is buzzing with ideas. • Encourages you to think thematically (helps find interesting links between ideas). • Helps you to see the 'bigger picture' and relationships. • Using colour coding helps to identify main themes, sub-themes and similar ideas. • Online tools aid quick and easy collaboration in group work. • Digital maps look neat and professional. • Digital maps are easy to correct.	• Some find them messy and visually confusing. • Can take practice/getting used to. • Hard to amend hand-drawn maps. • Space on a physical page can be limiting. • Space on a digital screen is even more limiting. Reducing text size makes them difficult to read. • Having secondary digital charts on different pages defeats the object – you can't see the bigger picture. • Online tools frustrate some as they introduce another 'layer' between the idea and the paper because the person is thinking about how to use the digital tool rather than the bigger ideas of their task.

 If you like to work on a larger scale, try using flipchart paper or wallpaper lining paper (much cheaper) to make enormous mind maps. You can cross through each area as you incorporate it into your final work.

Using AI to plan essays

Do you remember my caveat at the start of this book? Use AI with great caution and make sure that you are sticking to your educational institution's policy. Do not use AI if you are told not to. Students who ignore this can be investigated, suspended and ultimately thrown off their courses. That's far too high a price to pay.

The second risk with using AI is that sometimes it just doesn't produce anything useful or appropriate.

> **An example: when AI doesn't work**
>
> A sociology student is writing an essay on the difference between equity and equality. He finds a source with a good definition of equality and asks AI to paraphrase this. The word 'equality' is repeated twice in the source.
>
> The AI app changes the second use of the word 'equality' to 'equity', on the basis that it's generally considered poor writing style to keep repeating the same word. However, these words **do** have different meanings and the assignment requires the student to demonstrate an in-depth understanding of this. That means he will lose marks if he transfers the AI-generated text into his work.

However, AI can sometimes help to give an outline plan for straightforward assignments if you are stuck, providing a jumping-off point to start writing.

Here is an AI response to the following question:

Plan this essay: Compare and contrast religious symbolism used in Shakespeare's *Julius Caesar* and *Hamlet*.

1. Introduction

    a. background information on *Julius Caesar* and *Hamlet*

    b. brief explanation of religious symbolism in literature

    c. thesis statement (sum up your central argument or point of your work).

2. Religious symbolism in *Julius Caesar*

    a. the omens and supernatural events

    b. the reference to ancient Roman religion

    c. the role of destiny and the gods.

3. Religious symbolism in *Hamlet*

    a. the ghost of Hamlet's father

    b. the references to Christianity and the Bible

    c. the role of fate and divine intervention.

4. Comparison of religious symbolism in *Julius Caesar* and *Hamlet*

    a. similarities in the use of religious symbolism

    b. differences in the portrayal of religion

    c. how the use of religious symbolism contributes to the themes of the plays.

5. Conclusion

    a. recap of the similarities and differences in the use of religious symbolism

    b. the importance of religious symbolism in Shakespeare's plays

    c. final thoughts and implications for understanding the plays.

(Open.ai 08/05/2023)

This would probably set you off on your writing, which is no bad thing. However, I can see some potential pitfalls of this particular structure as someone who regularly marks students' work, which is that there is the potential for repetition in section 4. You would need to repeat some of the points you made earlier to make the comparison. This would probably be better as a thematic structure.

Stage four: writing a draft

You have written a comprehensive plan, so now you 'just' need to string all of your thoughts together into complete sentences, making sure that your key points and your arguments are clearly expressed and cohesive. This section gives you a series of pointers to help you with this.

 If you get stuck at this point, try recording yourself talking through your ideas for the essay, or have a discussion about it with a peer and record that (with their permission).

A key bit of advice here is to make sure that your audience knows where you are going. Remember that forest path analogy from earlier? We don't want them to feel lost in your writing.

Using signposting words and phrases

Signposting words and phrases are incredibly useful for your audience as they help to explain where you are heading and what readers should expect to be looking at next. Your structure will not make sense to your audience unless they understand it.

Signposting also helps to give a strong sense of cohesion to your work, making your argument clear and helping your writing feel like it 'flows'. Students gain marks for this.

Here are some useful signposting phrases.

To introduce a new idea	To introduce a contrasting idea
At the outset, it is useful to explain...	An alternative view is provided by...
To understand this issue, it is essential to define the key terms...	However,
The first and most crucial point is...	In contrast, [name] describes...
The second area of discussion is...	Conversely...
A further concept described is...	While [name] states [issue], the next author discussed has a different approach...
	Though,
	Despite this,
	Whereas...

To add further supporting points	Cause and effect
In addition,	As a result,
Further evidence is provided by...	Consequently,
Similarly...	Subsequently,
Corroborating evidence is provided by...	Therefore,
An extension of this idea is given by...	Thus,
Equally,	Accordingly,
	This results in...

Providing examples	Concluding
For example,	Finally,
That is,	In conclusion,
To illustrate,	To summarize,
A case in point is,	

 Add some signposting about your structure in your introduction; for example: 'This discussion will first explore the main themes of fate, religion and love.'

Paragraphing

You should write a new paragraph every time you introduce a new idea. Paragraphs generally start with some kind of topic sentence, again, so that your audience knows what to expect.

So, you should explain what you are talking about and add a signposting phrase so that your audience understands why you are introducing this new idea at this point. For example, a new paragraph might be:

(The paragraph before discusses religious symbolism as it relates to organized religion...)

> While it is apparent that the institution of the church is important in Shakespeare's writing, he also uses symbolism relating to the supernatural on several occasions. These areas are sometimes interwoven; for example,...(this paragraph continues to explain how less traditional ideas of religious symbolism, such as the supernatural, are included in Shakespeare's writing).

At the end of your paragraph, you should check that you can link your ideas back to the original question under discussion. If you cannot link the issue you have discussed back to this question, then you almost certainly don't need to include it – that goblin's on your shoulder again asking, 'Why should I care?' For example, the end of the paragraph which discusses the supernatural might finish along these lines:

> This evidence suggests that in Shakespeare's writing the supernatural and organized or institutional religion are deeply intertwined and engrained within his writing.

Making your argument

You are always stating a case when you are writing academically. To do this effectively, you must explain yourself clearly and provide evidence. Here are a couple of different ways of reminding yourself to do this.

The first has been around for a long time and is known as PEEL (Point, Evidence, Explanation, Link). There are advantages to this approach as it is quite straightforward.

It can work very well for subjects which are fact based and do not have a huge amount of inference built in **as long as you remember** to link back to your question.

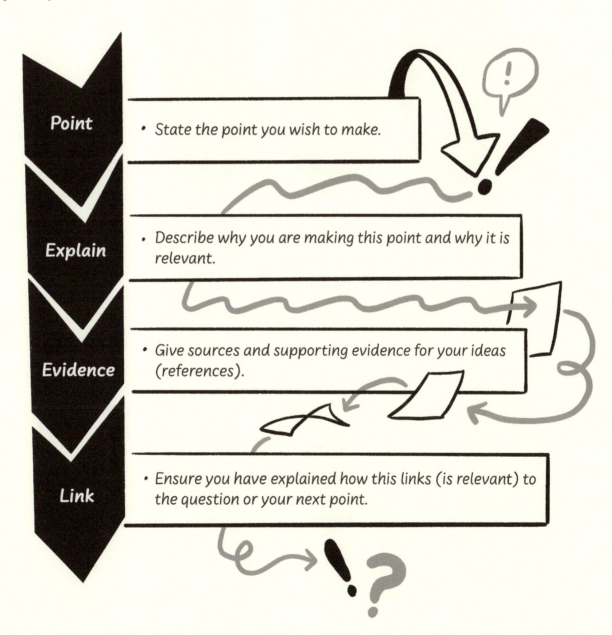

- **Point** — State the point you wish to make.
- **Explain** — Describe why you are making this point and why it is relevant.
- **Evidence** — Give sources and supporting evidence for your ideas (references).
- **Link** — Ensure you have explained how this links (is relevant) to the question or your next point.

An alternative, more nuanced approach is to use **what, why and how** as writing prompts for yourself. This works well for subjects where there is often the need for increased inference, such as in English literature and history.

Here is an example:

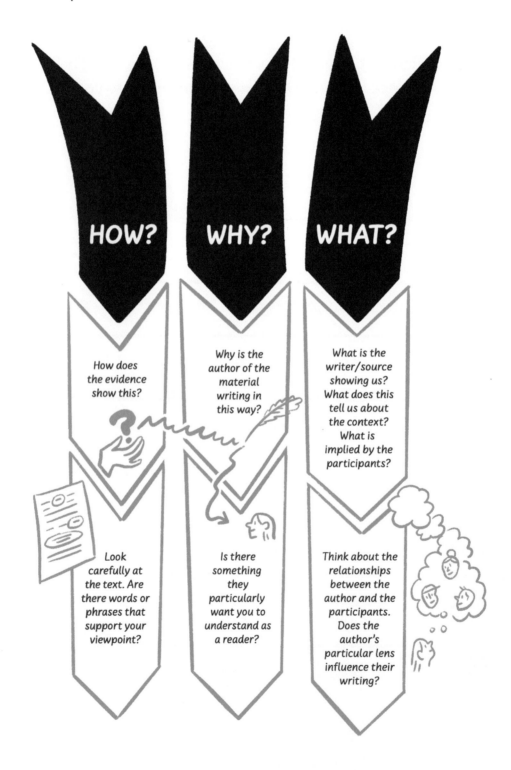

Choosing your language to support your point

Every time you make a claim you will usually be giving some supporting evidence. The evidence you describe may be strong or weak. You will be evaluating how relevant it is to your argument. You can choose your language carefully so that your audience clearly understands your position.

Using **evaluative language** helps you to make this argument, enabling you to state your critical position concerning your essay question. Evaluative phrases help you to express your opinion and include positive, negative or neutral words. These are particularly useful to include in your linking or signposting phrases.

You might emphasize your argument by using powerful verbs and adverbs, using phrases like: '**clearly** demonstrates' and '**unquestionably** explains'. Here your reader is in no doubt that you are entirely certain about your claim.

> *Verbs are the main action (or feeling) in a sentence; for example, she **loved** him.*
>
> *Adverbs add information to verbs. They describe how an action (or feeling is carried out); for example, she loved him **unconditionally**.*

On the next page is a table of some handy evaluative phrases, including some optional adverbs that can be used to emphasize your viewpoint.

Evaluative verbs	Optional adverbs	Example sentence usage
implies	accurately	Smith (2023) accurately implies that the research undertaken cannot be considered conclusive due to the small sample size.
suggests	somewhat	This somewhat suggests a link between the two issues.
indicates	strongly	This strongly indicates a degree of confusion.
expands	surely	The author surely expands upon the points made by previous researchers.
develops	fully	This work fully develops the initial principles first introduced by Davies and Hind (1910) in the early 20th century.
considers	carefully	The researchers carefully consider this issue.
contradicts	unequivocally	The character's second statement on the issue unequivocally contradicts his viewpoint expressed in the previous chapter.
concludes	clearly	This clearly concludes that further research is needed in this area before the issue can be resolved.
highlights	questionably	This questionably highlights how participants felt pressured by research.
relates	possibly	This angry statement possibly relates to the earlier issue of sibling rivalry.
contrasts	marginally	This marginally contrasts with the evidence provided in previous research.
compares	fairly	This fairly compares the roles of landowners in Scotland to those of New South Wales in the 19th century.
criticizes	unusually	Unusually, this criticizes the most common approaches to such issues.
introduces	conversely	Conversely, this introduces an alternative perspective on the issue at hand.
influences	noticeably	This early work noticeably influences writers such as Hemingway.

explains	simply	This study simply explains the relationship between the developing industrial landscape and economic power.
expresses	undoubtedly	The author undoubtedly expresses her support for these issues through the use of emotive language.
supports	fully	This fully supports the earlier research by Davies.
connects	unquestionably	This work unquestionably connects issues relating to the role of women in politics and wider structural inequalities.
illustrates	theoretically	This theoretically illustrates the importance of the role of health care in this context.
provides	evidently	This study evidently provides a valuable alternative perspective on the issue.
achieves	cleverly	The author cleverly achieves this effect by using complex metaphors.
exemplifies	vividly	This vividly exemplifies how participatory research can shed new light on issues which have been considered to have been exhausted by previous studies.

Hedging

Sometimes you are not so sure about your claim or the evidence only partially supports your point. This is an opportunity to use the language of suggestion or possibility (sometimes known as hedging language). Some examples are:

* It is likely that...
* This indicates...
* This could be attributed to...
* It is probable that...
* It may...

In this way, the reader can see that you are qualifying your ideas and have thought carefully about the strength of the evidence. Be careful not to use hedging instead of finding good sources and using clear referencing, though!

Writing succinctly: summarizing and paraphrasing

Once you have found the source material for your essay, it is very important to present this in a way that is succinct and accessible to your readers.

> *Writing succinctly: being short and to the point without including unnecessary words.*

This means you must be able to summarize and paraphrase the information accurately, always keeping in mind the 'why' so that your audience understands the relevance of your words.

Summarizing

Writing a summary allows you to show that you have fully understood an idea or argument. You can use the SQ3R method to read critically if you like it (see Chapter 6).

> *Summarizing: explaining an idea in a shortened form.*

The important thing here is to ensure that you have fully understood the text because you need to be able to condense the ideas into a much shorter piece of writing. In practice, we usually combine our summarizing and paraphrasing skills.

Paraphrasing

> *Paraphrasing: putting text into your own words, without changing the meaning.*

You absolutely **must** use your own words in academic writing. This is particularly important at college and university levels as most institutions will run your work through anti-plagiarism software. This gives an estimated score relating to the amount of material it believes you to have copied.

The first three stages of paraphrasing are:

1. Read and understand the source writing.

2. Underline the key points.

3. Highlight any words that you do not already know alternatives for and find synonyms for these.

Using synonyms in your writing is very useful. You can find them in a thesaurus, and most word-processing software has built-in thesaurus functions. You can also ask the internet to give you a synonym. However, you should be careful that the synonym suggested does not change the meaning of a sentence.

> *Synonyms: words or phrases that mean exactly or almost the same as another word within a phrase or sentence.*

> **Example: take care when choosing synonyms**
>
> A student asked a search engine to find a synonym for the word 'close' in the following sentence:
>
> 'The participants were **close** to the researchers which may have influenced their responses.'
>
> The search engine suggested replacing 'close' with the word 'shut'. However, this would make zero sense in this phrase!
>
> The word 'known to', or a description of their relationship, would have been more accurate.

Here is a useful list of some common synonyms for academic writing.

Original	Synonym/s	Original	Synonym/s
research	study, work	**evaluates**	analyses
considers	discusses	**explains**	describes
evidences	illustrates	**highlights**	underlines
limitation	restriction	**similar**	comparable, alike
reveals	exposes	**demonstrates**	shows
important	substantial	**concurs**	agrees
contrast	alternative	**conflicts**	contrasts

You can take a step-by-step approach to paraphrasing your work once you have found your synonyms.

Completing Assignments, Essays and Dissertations

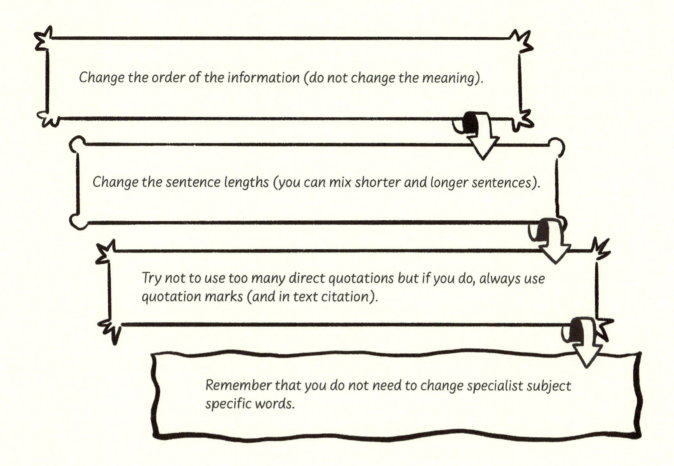

Change the order of the information (do not change the meaning).

Change the sentence lengths (you can mix shorter and longer sentences).

Try not to use too many direct quotations but if you do, always use quotation marks (and in text citation).

Remember that you do not need to change specialist subject specific words.

Paraphrasing example

Let's imagine that you are required to analyse this first paragraph of Sherlock Holmes's story, 'The Adventure of the Mazarin Stone':[3]

> It was pleasant to Doctor Watson to find himself once more in the untidy room of the first floor in Baker Street which had been the starting point of so many remarkable adventures. He looked around him at the scientific charts upon the wall, the acid-charred bench of chemicals, the violin-case leaning in the corner, the coal-scuttle, which contained of old the pipes and tobacco. Finally, his eyes came round to the fresh and smiling face of Billy, the young but very wise and tactful page, who had helped a little to fill up the gap of loneliness and isolation which surrounded the **saturnine** figure of the great detective.

183

Paraphrasing stage	Comment
Read and understand the writing.	It is the opening paragraph. It is setting the scene. It's messy but familiar (both physical space and people within it).
Underline the key points.	Doctor Watson is back and happy about it. Billy is still there too. The room looks unchanged. Sherlock is still lonely and isolated.
Highlight any unknown words and find synonyms.	Saturnine. Synonyms: melancholy or gloomy.

> We can just paraphrase this in a straightforward way:
>
> > Doctor Watson was pleased to return to the disordered room on the first floor of Baker Street, where numerous extraordinary adventures had begun. He surveyed the room, noting the scientific charts hanging on the walls, the chemical-stained workbench, the violin-case resting in the corner, and the coal-scuttle which still held pipes and tobacco. Finally, his gaze settled on the cheerful countenance of Billy, the young yet astute and diplomatic aide, who had somewhat assisted in reducing the loneliness and seclusion which encircled the melancholy great detective.
>
> Note the use of several synonyms. However, this is still very long-winded and is probably not what would be required for an essay on this piece of work.

Let's see what it might look like if we summarize it too, making it more succinct and explaining **the purpose** of the paragraph. Think back to the **What, How, Why?** idea from earlier in this chapter.

> The opening paragraph effectively sets the scene and introduces the main characters of Doctor Watson, Billy (the assistant) and Sherlock Holmes. Conan-Doyle uses Doctor Watson's gaze to remind readers of the setting and the key protagonists as he effectively surveys the room; reintroducing the audience to individual characteristics of the physical context and the personalities within it. This description helps to establish a sense of cosy

familiarity which is reinforced by the use of everyday language by the characters. We are reminded that Holmes remains a melancholy figure, while Billy is resolutely cheerful. Watson himself is pleased to be back in this apparently disordered environment. Conan-Doyle emphasizes that it has been the 'starting point' of many an adventure, creating a sense of anticipation and an eagerness for the story to commence.

 If you are writing a longer piece, perhaps a dissertation or end-of-course assignment, create a second document titled something like, 'stuff I've cut out'. Use the same chapter headings. When you are editing, you cut and paste unwanted material into this document under the corresponding chapter headings. You never know when you might need to go back and use it again.

Using academic language

Attitudes towards what is and is not accepted in academic writing are continuing to evolve. This is not surprising because language use constantly adapts and updates according to our context. Think about all of the words that we now use that our ancestors would have used very differently. My grandparents only knew 'the web' as something made by spiders!

My impression is that writing generally is becoming less formal. However, for the time being, at least, most academic writing remains very formal, with the idea that the work should come across as being objective and considered.

In summary, academic writers:

* choose words which are formal and subject specific

* generally, try to write in the third person where possible, for example, 'It is considered...' Or use the topic as the subject of their writing, 'Research in this area is inconclusive as...'

You can help your work to sound more academic if you **avoid** these things:

* using informal words or expressions, so that means no slang or idioms (phrases like 'he took his eye off the ball')
* using hyperbole – this is what we call exaggerated language like 'It took forever to write this'
* using contractions – so you would write 'It cannot be the case' rather than 'It can't be the case'
* writing in the first person (avoid using 'I')
* using 'you' (as in 'you will see that I am writing about…')
* using 'we' (as in 'we will now look at the issue…') – there is only one of you!
* using rhetorical questions (questions that do not need an answer).

Here are some examples.

Original, poor example	Improved example
Which approach is better when we are thinking about social justice and inequality? I will compare two approaches and discuss which is more meaningful.	This assignment considers two contrasting approaches to the ideas of social justice and equality. It compares both and discusses which is more meaningful.
I find it really peculiar that pupils with the highest needs often have the least teacher time.	It seems unusual that pupils with the highest needs often have the least input from teachers.
It can't be a coincidence that sales skyrocketed after the celebrity was seen wearing that product.	It cannot be coincidental that sales significantly increased after the celebrity was seen wearing the product.

Reflective writing

Quite often we are asked to reflect on our learning. You might be required to describe what you found interesting or challenging and to evaluate your learning experiences. Here you can:

* use the first person, 'I' to give your views
* still write formally (it's for academic purposes)
* avoid using conversational language or phrasing.

Writing online blogs and forums

Increasingly, courses seem to be incorporating writing on blogs or forums as part of assessment criteria. Finding an appropriate tone for writing here can be tricky. I generally advise students to try to keep reasonably formal, even though we are usually very familiar in tone (particularly on forums). It's best to check your assessment criteria carefully and to look carefully at any examples your tutor may have given you. In particular, watch out for any referencing requirements, as these are often needed even though they are not something you would typically see in an online blog or forum posting.

Group work assignments

Often students are required to work in small groups as part of their assignment criteria, commonly to create a presentation of some kind. You can find tips on giving effective presentations in Chapter 9 'Oral Skills'. Here, I am going to discuss some of the issues that arise in group work.

First, I am frustrated when neurodivergent students, particularly those with autism in their profiles, are characterized as being 'bad' at group work. In my experience, this is more about a lack of control of the process and the often lackadaisical approach taken by some of their neurotypical peers! This can leave students feeling very frustrated and stressed.

My main advice is to ensure that there are very clearly defined roles within the group and that every meeting held has an agenda. This can help keep moving processes forward.

> **Group work example**
>
> A group of four students studying health and social care must choose a case study and make a presentation which describes the impact of a recent national health policy intervention. This is their agenda for their first meeting:
>
> 1. Agree their chosen case study.
>
> 2. Allocate the following roles: coordinating chair (this person sets up meetings and provides the agenda) and editor (the person who pulls together everyone's ideas and makes the presentation look cohesive).
>
> 3. Allocate topics to individuals (remembering that the chair and editor should have the easiest or smallest topic areas, given they will be spending time on their other roles).
>
> 4. Agree deadlines for first drafts.
>
> 5. Agree a date for next meeting.
>
> 6. Agree outline agenda for next meeting (chair will distribute prior and ask for additions).

Managing these roles and deadlines can be tricky, particularly if another group member does not seem to be taking the task very seriously. This is one of the most difficult things to deal with. On one hand, students do not want to get a peer in trouble by telling their teacher or lecturer. On the other, they do not want to get a bad result because of someone else's lack of effort.

A student might decide to tackle their peer head-on and tell them they are not pulling their weight. This is legitimate, but there are ways of doing this to avoid confrontation. One tactic is to avoid using the word 'you' when you are trying to get things sorted, as it can feel a bit like someone is pointing their finger.

Let me give an example to show you what I mean:

> 'You aren't giving us your slides when you are supposed to and so you are going to get us all marked down.'

or

> **'I am worried that we won't get a good mark because we aren't getting the slides on time.'**

Can you see how the tone is very different in the bold text? It is much less accusatory and less personal. If you are comfortable trying that, it might be worth a shot. If that doesn't work, then I think it is a good idea to let your teacher/tutor know that you are having difficulties as they will often take this into account when marking.

 If you are working on a problem-solving group assignment, you can try using an Ishikawa diagram from Chapter 4. This can give you something objective to focus on as a group and is a good jumping-off point for ideas.

Referencing

This subject often makes students groan. Referencing can feel very onerous and complicated. However, once you get into the swing of it, it can be surprisingly straightforward.

The first thing to say is to be careful to follow whichever referencing system your educational institution recommends. I will use Harvard Cite Them Right as an example system here, just because it is commonly used. There are others, though, and law students in particular will use a different style altogether.

Why do we need to reference?

Referencing shows your reader that you have used a wide range of different sources to support your evidence or argument. It demonstrates your understanding of the subject. It highlights the role of other people's work in your assignment and allows your readers to check the validity of your claims. Vitally, it helps you to avoid accusations of plagiarism.

What do we need to reference?

You need to reference any information that would not be considered common knowledge. For example, you would not need to reference the statement: 'London is the capital of England.' However, you would need to provide a reference if you wrote: 'Greater London is the most urbanized area in the UK.'

Types of referencing for assignments

There are two main types of referencing for assignments:

1. In-text citation. These are not complete references. They 'sit' within your writing and give just enough information for your reader to be able to find the full reference at the end of your work.

2. The full reference list which you provide at the end of your writing. This is very detailed and should allow your reader to easily find the sources of your information.

In-text citation

It is usually enough to give the author's name and the date of their work here. Generally, you can list up to three authors. If there are more than three, you would use the first author's name and 'et al.' which is just an abbreviation of the Latin phrase 'et alia' meaning 'and others'.

Example:
While few would argue against the principle of universal rights to free education,

Shaw (2021) explores the last half century of progress towards inclusion for disabled students within higher education. The findings describe multiple barriers based upon inaccurate representations of disability, both in the past and present-day (Shaw, 2021).

End of assignment referencing

This is much more detailed. If you are studying in higher education, you will almost certainly have access to a library and many sources will be online. Here there is usually a button to click on which will be named something like 'citation'. Very handily, these give you the full citation that you will need for your work. You would just need to add the date that you accessed the information.

Example:

Shaw, A. (2021) 'Inclusion of disabled Higher Education students: why are we not there yet?', *International Journal of Inclusive Education*, 28(6), pp. 820–838. doi: 10.1080/13603116.2021.1968514 (Accessed: 20 May 2025).

What's a bibliography then?

A bibliography is a list of everything you have read in connection with your writing and can include work that you haven't actually included in your assignment. Not many universities require bibliographies to be included at the undergraduate level. This is something to check with your tutors if they ask you to include one.

Referencing software/apps

Using these can be hugely helpful, particularly as you progress through your studies and accumulate huge amounts of source material. You can 'tag' your readings and save your source documents under different tabs, thereby organizing your research thematically.

Tagging example

A student is writing about disability rights. They decide on the themes they are interested in and create a series of tags to 'attach' to each piece of reading they complete: history of disability rights, legislation, activism and future developments.

This makes it much easier to locate relevant texts when it comes to writing up their work.

There are many different options available. Two common referencing systems used by my students are Zotero and Mendeley. Both allow you to choose the citation system required by your institution and will create in-text citations and end references accordingly. It is well worth taking some time to explore such software to see if it will help you organize your reading and speed up the referencing process.

Librarians in schools, colleges and universities are fantastic sources of help and advice. Often, they have online tutorials to talk you through how to reference and how to use digital referencing tools. It is worth spending an hour looking at these as it will save you lots of time later!

Stage four: proofreading

The final stage before submission is to check your work very carefully for errors in spelling, punctuation, grammar and formatting. It is very easy to lose marks here and, as a marker, I find it frustrating when I have to dock points for mistakes which should be easily correctable. However, the word 'easily' in my last sentence is doing a lot of work! Proofreading is a skill and one that needs practice. It can be particularly challenging for those of you with dyslexia in your profile. Students are also doing this at the point when they are usually heartily fed up with the work they have been slogging through and they just want to send it in.

There are some tips and tricks that can help you with this:

* **Use spelling and grammar checkers.** This is probably obvious. However, you should use them with care as they can be unreliable, particularly when it comes to identifying the difference between US and UK spelling conventions.

- **Read it aloud.** This is by far my favourite method. If you read it aloud you will most likely hear when sentences don't make sense, or you will stumble over misspellings. It might not work so well if you are dyslexic as you may read your spellings as correct. If this applies to you, use the 'read aloud' feature to read it to you (available under 'accessibility features' for most software). The reading software will misread incorrect spelling which will naturally jar your ears!

- **Print it out or change the font/colour.** If we keep looking at the same document in the same format, it can be harder to spot mistakes. You might be able to find them more easily if you can print your work. Alternatively, you can try changing the font and/or colour of your text to give your eyes a 'fresh' text to read.

- **Leave time between finishing and checking.** Walk away and leave your document, ideally overnight. Your eyes and brain will be refreshed.

- **Read specifically for your bugbears.** For example, if you know that you always confuse 'where' and 'were', you can look specifically for this.

- **Ask a friend to look over your work.**

 You can use 'find and replace' features in Word and Google Docs. This is a very quick way of correcting repeated mistakes; for example, if you have misspelt someone's surname throughout your document.

Using text-to-speech to help with writing

Speech-to-text and text-to-speech have come on leaps and bounds in recent years, and there is now a wide range of options to try when writing your assignments. This can be particularly helpful for students with dysgraphia and/or dyslexia in their profiles, as these students often have strong verbal skills but can find the process of writing difficult and frustrating.

Common operating systems like Google and Microsoft have excellent free tools. There is also custom software available with advanced capabilities. This can be expensive but also very useful. There are versions which have built-in specialist vocabulary for certain subjects such as medicine and law. If you think this would help you, I would advise you to speak to your additional needs team at your school, college or university. Sometimes funding is available. It can take a bit of getting used to but can work very well. I wrote much of this book using speech-to-text! You might also be able to use it in exams, particularly if it's something you use regularly in class as it may well be counted as a reasonable adjustment. Just check with the person or team responsible for exams, well ahead of time, so that they can make sure for you.

 When using speech-to-text, remember to check your work carefully for more informal phrasing, particularly the use of contractions such as it's and they're. These are not considered suitable for academic writing but will not usually be highlighted by spelling and grammar checkers.

Dissertation specific points

Most final-year university or college students will be required to write a dissertation as part of their course. If you're not there yet, you can skip this section!

*A **dissertation** is a research project. You investigate a question you have written yourself and then present your findings. At university degree and college level, these are usually 5000 to 8000 words long.*

All of the advice given in this chapter so far works for dissertation writing too, but there are some specific things that you will need to think about which don't usually apply when writing other kinds of assignments or coursework.

Writing your question

Usually, you will be writing your own question for your dissertation. This can be very difficult for all students, particularly so for neurodivergent learners. I think this is because there can be a fear of missing something out or somehow getting 'the wrong end of the stick'.

My best advice here is to work closely with your tutor or supervisor when writing your question. However, there are some general tips to think about:

* Pick something that interests you. You will be spending a lot of time on this!

* Don't be too broad when you decide on the area you will be looking at. This is an opportunity to delve more deeply.

* Use words which invite an open debate rather than a closed answer. Let me explain what I mean:

    'To what extent has legislation affected livestock movement in the past decade?'

    Is better than:

    'Has legalization stopped livestock movement in the past decade?'

That helps you to try to keep an open mind about what your dissertation might discover. So, try not to frame your question as a foregone conclusion.

Dissertation contents

This will usually comprise (see the next page):

Section	Contents
Abstract	Helps readers see at a glance what you have written about. Briefly state: • your key question • your methodology • key findings and conclusion.
Introduction	• Say what you will be writing about. • Explain any key terminology. • Say why it is a worthwhile area to explore. • Explain the range of your study (what is included and what isn't and remember to say why you have made this decision). • State what methodology you are using. • Signpost the structure.
Literature review	• Critically examines a selection of sources which relate to the topic you are exploring. • Shows current thinking in the area. • You demonstrate your understanding of the issues by comparing and contrasting these ideas. • You might also identify gaps in current knowledge.
Methodology	• Describes the methods you have decided to use to collect your information/data. • Explains in detail why you have chosen these methods. • Details the practicalities of how this took place, including things like consents obtained, location of any interviews etc.
Results	• Your findings. • Present your data here. You might be using diagrams, charts, tables and graphs in this section.
Discussion	• Talk about your findings here. • Analyse them in detail. • Point out any gaps or anomalies. • Look for themes or relationships and highlight these. • Remember to explain how these relate to your original question.
Conclusion	• Link this back to your original question. • Explain to what extent you have been able to answer it. • Summarize the key findings. • State whether there is any further research that could help throw light on your own.

Thinking about your data collection methodology: quantitative or qualitative (or mixed)?

There are lots of different ways of collecting information for research, and so this section briefly summarizes only the most common ones you will find at the undergraduate level.

You will need to decide what kind of research and data you will collect to help you investigate your question. This broadly fits into two categories: quantitative and qualitative.

> *Quantitative* research is fully measurable. Your findings will be based on countable data and solid facts.
>
> *Qualitative* research is more descriptive. Your results will be open to interpretation, though still based on your findings. These can help to shed light on why certain situations or behaviours arise.

Whether you choose quantitative or qualitative methods will be driven by your subject. For example, a student studying chemistry is likely to be testing a hypothesis which can be fully measured (so it will be a quantitative study). A different student may be doing a sociology degree and looking at experiences of growing up in a multicultural area. Her research will be qualitative.

Some students will do a mixture of both methods (mixed methods research). For example, the sociology student might do a series of interviews to gather information, which will be qualitative data. She might also collect some quantitative (measurable) data such as her participants' ages, incomes and levels of education.

Writing literature reviews

This is something that most students find difficult and they can be tricky. Literature reviews form a crucial part of dissertation writing.

> **A literature review** critically examines a selection of sources which relate to the topic you are exploring. It shows current thinking in the area. You demonstrate your understanding of the issues by comparing and contrasting these ideas. You might also identify gaps in current knowledge.

Again, talk to your tutor or dissertation supervisor to find out exactly what your institution requires from you, but here are some of the typical first steps to take:

* Find out how many sources you need to include. This will vary depending on where you are studying, but generally, it is better to look at a few in great depth rather than pick too many and produce a superficial overview.

* Find your literature. Look back at the section on using libraries and conducting online research.

* Remember to avoid confirmation bias and try to find works which are up to date. Make sure that you check the validity of your sources. That means looking at where they are published and being sure they have been peer-reviewed (so, not just opinion pieces).

Once you have found your sources you need to critically read them.

 While you are reading, you can start to think about how you can structure your review. Look at the section below 'Structuring your literature review' now before you start reading.

What should I be looking for when I am reading each piece of literature?

Here are some key questions to keep in mind when you are reading. You could put these questions into a table to help you keep track of your thoughts and to make sure that you are interrogating each source thoroughly.

1. What did this research want to find out?

2. Did it find out what it wanted to? Why?

3. What is their perspective (do they use a particular theory, or do they have a certain 'lens' – their view on the world)?

4. What is the research method?

5. Are the methods used appropriate (think about reliability and accuracy)?

6. How valid is their argument based on their findings?

7. Can you find any gaps or limitations?

8. Is this research the same/different to other research you've found about your topic? How/why?

9. What does this tell you about your subject?

You can use this table to record your questions and thoughts.

Source name	Topic/theme	Link or reference
What's it trying to find out?		
Did it find out what it wanted to? Why?		
What is the perspective/theological stance?		
What research methods are used?		
Are research methods appropriate/reliable/valid?		
Are the findings valid based on evidence?		
Any gaps or limitations?		
Same or different to other research? How/why?		
What does this tell you about your subject?		

Structuring your literature review

Start by deciding how you would like to sort your information (the readings and so on that you have found). There are different ways of doing this.

Sort by	What is this?	What's it good for?
Chronology	In order of the date published.	Subjects where there is a clear timeline of the development of ideas.
Theme	Group sources with similar ideas together.	Works well when you are comparing and contrasting ideas between authors who share similar views. Often the choice for qualitative studies.
Methodological approach	The stance they took when deciding what method/s they have used to collect data.	Good for more quantitative studies when you are looking at measurable data. Also relevant for qualitative studies, particularly if you can see potential issues in methodology and data collection.
Theoretical approach	This is the philosophical standpoint of the author.	Useful when there are clearly defined 'schools of thought' about a subject/topic as you can group authors accordingly.

 Why not colourcode your sources? For example, use a different colour for different themes. It will help you to sort your ideas quickly.

Now, you just need to write it up! You can use the principles from the other chapters of this book to help you with that.

We have looked in quite some detail at different kinds of written assessments in this chapter, but lots of courses also have exams of one kind or other to complete. That's what the next chapter will look at.

Let's recap

In this chapter we have covered:

- dissertation specific points.
- writing as a process
- using feedback to improve
- understanding the question
- selecting what information and content to include
- making a plan
- deciding on structure
- four popular planning techniques
- mind-mapping tech
- using AI to plan
- writing a draft
- signposting words and phrases
- paraphrasing
- making your argument
- choosing language to support your point
- writing succinctly
- using academic English
- reflective writing
- group work assignments
- referencing
- proofreading
- speech-to-text tech.

Key takeaway points from this chapter

- Writing is a process. You need to work through each stage of that process to be a successful academic writer.

- Remember to use feedback to improve your work.

- Try different methods of planning until you find one you like.

- Choose your words carefully to fit the purpose and audience.

- You need to have a consistent 'story' for your work.

- Make sure that everything you say is linked and relevant to your question and argument.

Chapter 8

ACHIEVING YOUR GOALS IN EXAMS

First, while exams are certainly important, they are never the **most** important thing. **Your health and wellbeing always come first**. This becomes even more crucial when you are under pressure. Remember to include lots of breaks and to play to any sensory preferences that you may have so that you can build in some soothing or lighter moments into your revision and exam periods.

 Please revisit the second chapter of this book for more guidance on self-care, and always ask a trusted person for help if you are feeling under too much stress.

Reasonable adjustments

Remember that many neurodivergent students are entitled to reasonable adjustments (sometimes known as accommodations) in exams, such as extra time, a quieter room, rest breaks etc. You can check this with your examinations officer or additional needs/disability team in your educational institution. Please ensure you are getting the support you are entitled to.

The importance of equity

Adjustments and accommodations in examinations are provided to give equity. This acknowledges that students do not all start from an equal position and so they need some kind of support to level the playing field from the start. Some students tell me they feel 'bad' for having extra time, or that 'it feels like cheating'. It **really** isn't. This is all about trying to make systems fairer and this is most definitely a good thing.

Reasonable adjustments help to provide equity. Everyone now has the same chance of success.

While exams can be daunting for everyone and even more so for neurodivergent students, there are several things you can do to make yourself more comfortable, and to help improve your chances of a good outcome.

Revision planning

There is usually a period of study leave before exams. This can be tricky if you thrive on routine because your usual weekly structure is thrown up in the air. Equally, it can encourage a chaotic approach if you naturally tend towards disorder! That means I would strongly encourage you to impose some kind of **routine and rhythm** upon yourself during study leave. This is particularly important if your study leave stretches over an extended period.

 You can use all of the time management techniques described in Chapter 3 'Getting Organized', with some extra steps, given that you are in revision mode.

There are many different ways of structuring your revision and your preferred method will depend on how much routine and control you like to have over your time. You can think of this as being a little like a layered pyramid. You can decide which level of detail most suits you.

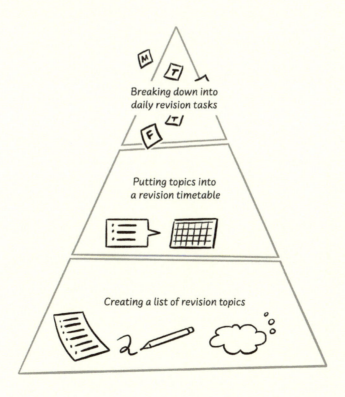

1. Creating a list of revision topics

The most basic way of planning revision is to create a list of topics for each subject that you need to cover.

* Tick each topic on your list as you cover it.

* Try to cover each subject three times (in different ways). That is to ensure that the information has a better chance of 'fixing' into your long-term memory.

* Colour code your revision to match any coding you have used throughout the year.

Example: a law student's revision list

Revision topic to cover (tick each time covered)	1	2	3
Medical law	✓		
Environmental law	✓		
Commercial law			
Family law	✓	✓	

Here's a blank copy of this revision list table.

Revision topic to cover (tick each time covered)	1	2	3

Listing like this means you can be very flexible and learn anything from the list whenever you want to as long as you cover everything three times. However, it does not prioritize subjects and makes no consideration for the timing of exams.

2. Putting topics into a more detailed revision timetable

To take the idea of your list a step further, you might like to transfer your revision subjects into a timetable, which includes your exams. You can colour code or shade this by subject.

You will see from the example below that there is some time off built into the programme. I have also assumed that this student will take regular breaks throughout the day and will not study in the evenings. I like to remind my students that they are not machines!

wk	Monday	Tuesday	Wednesday	Thursday	Friday	Saturday	Sunday
1	Commercial Law	Family Law	Environmental Law	Day off	Medical Law	Medical Law	Environmental Law
		Afternoon off					
2	Environmental Law	**EXAM** **Environmental Law**	Medical Law	**EXAM** **Medical Law**	Day off	Commercial Law	Commercial Law
3	**EXAM** **Commercial Law**	Morning off	Family Law	Family Law	**EXAM** **Family Law**	Celebrate the end of exams!	
		Family Law afternoon					

Here is blank copy of a weekly planning table for one month of study.

wk		Monday	Tuesday	Wednesday	Thursday	Friday	Saturday	Sunday
1	am							
	pm							
2	am							
	pm							
3	am							
	pm							
4	am							
	pm							

Interleaving topics

You will see that in all the examples I have used, the subjects are mainly interleaved. This means that you are mixing your subjects across the revision period rather than completing topics in blocks. This looks messy, but there are advantages to doing it this way, particularly when you have several exams:

* It limits the risk of forgetting the subject that you revised first.
* It helps to keep your interest, as doing consecutive days of the same subject can be mind-numbing.
* It reduces the risk of running out of time and not being able to cover the final subject on your list at all.
* Spaced repetition[1] of learning has been shown to help information embed in your memory.[2]

However, for some students, this timetable is still too vague and they might find they do not know where to start on each given day.

Breaking topics down into daily tasks

You can make a daily list of things you want to revise and this can be very helpful for some. Others will find this far too constraining and will become frustrated if they cannot stick exactly to the list they have predetermined for themselves! Therefore, the level of detail that you include here is very personal.

 This is good for building in 'set times' for self-care which is sensible if you get stressed or anxious during revision and exams.

Here is a daily revision planning example based on the first two days of the law student's study leave.

	Monday	**Tuesday**
09.30	Commercial Law – lectures 1 to 3	Family Law – lectures 1 to 2
10.30	Tea break	Tea break
11.00	Commercial Law – lectures 4 to 7	Family Law – lectures 3 to 4
12.00	Lunch break (walk around local park)	Lunch break
13.00	Commercial Law – lectures 8 to 11	Family Law – lectures 5 to 6
14.00	Tea break	Review Commercial Law lectures 1 to 3
14.30	Commercial Law – lectures 12 to 15	Meet a friend for a coffee
16.00	Finish for the day	
Evening	Video gaming	Go for a swim

You can adapt your timetable according to your own needs. For example, this student enjoys commercial law and so decides they can get through lots of revision on Monday. However, they find family law quite hard to digest so are only aiming to revise two lectures an hour for this subject.

 Here's the daily planning revision table to use.

	Monday	*Tuesday*
09.30		
10.30		
11.00		
12.00	*Lunch break*	*Lunch break*
13.30		
14.00		
14.30	*Tea break*	*Tea break*
15.00		

	Monday	Tuesday
15.30		
16.00		
Evening	Joyful activity	Joyful activity

Having a plan B

What happens if you simply can't face the next topic on your carefully written revision plan? This happens to everyone sometimes, and this could be for all sorts of reasons. Often, it's because we are just a bit fed up with the same subject, are tired or feel somewhat 'stuck' on a topic that we find difficult. If this happens it is much better to move on to something else rather than sit staring at your work, feeling guilty that you are not doing what you are 'supposed to'.

This is why I often advise students to have a 'plan B' list, ready to use for these situations, which means writing it up **before** you begin the revision period. This could be a simple 'tick-list' of things to look at. So, it could be a list of recorded lectures to review or some chapters of subject-related books to read. Doing something else productive can help to break any feelings of frustration which have been building up.

 You could also try some of the strategies listed in Chapter 4 'Overcoming Barriers to Learning – Avoiding Procrastination'.

Time management during revision periods

I have mentioned before that you must take regular breaks. This is very important as it helps to keep your mind active and your body moving. It is vital during exam periods. The most popular strategy is the **Pomodoro Technique.**[3]

The Pomodoro Technique

This strategy takes its name from the Italian word for tomato. That's because its originator, Francesco Cirillo, used a tomato-shaped kitchen timer to manage his time.

The Pomodoro Technique breaks study periods into short chunks, followed by short breaks. You can use a physical timer, or the timer on your phone, or there are apps which use the same principle.

It works like this:

1. Set a timer for 25 minutes of study.

2. Take a five-minute break when the timer goes off.

3. Repeat this a total of four times.

4. Take a longer break (around half an hour).

5. Repeat.

This strategy can help students to stay mentally fresh and sustain study for longer periods. I have found that students with ADHD in their profile find it works particularly well, especially if they remember to physically move during the five-minute breaks.

All *students should try to do something different in the break – step away from their laptop, make a cup of tea or have a stretch.*

However, some students find that an arbitrary timer of 25 minutes breaks their concentration entirely, sometimes when they are in the middle of a topic which they are enjoying and studying effectively. So, while I would always encourage you to have regular breaks, you can adapt the timings to suit yourself. It is definitely something that needs experimentation to find a pattern which works for you, though I would never recommend studying for over an hour without a break. You can also think of this being like **time-boxing** – giving yourself a window of time when you decide that you will be studying a certain subject.

 It's okay to stray from your plan. If you are stuck on a subject and the information just isn't 'going in', it is better to move on to something else.

Revision methods

There is an enormous range of revision methods to try out. Research[4] can help guide us towards the most effective strategies. Broadly speaking, the more proactive the study activity is, the more effective it will be. Equally, building variety into your revision methods will help to support your recall of information.[5] That means you should do the following:

* Interleave your study topics – that means mixing up your topics and weaving them into a pattern rather than doing one topic in a block before moving on to the next one.

* Choose a selection of different methods to revise each topic – do not attempt to passively read! Try to actively ask questions of yourself and the material you are reading.

* Try to vary the context/how you are actually revising. For example, you might study in the library one day, or at home the next. You can also change your physical position. Try standing up to revise, or walk around and say information aloud to remind yourself of key facts.

* In general, remember to physically move and take regular breaks.

Coming up next are several different revision strategies that you can try. See if you can find two or three that work for you so that you can build in that variety I have been talking about!

Making revision notes

Making effective revision notes can be tricky. Often, students worry they will over-summarize and leave out important details. Others say they struggle to identify the key points.

> *If you have used one of the note-taking methods mentioned in Chapter 5 'Managing in Class and Note-taking in Lectures', you will have a head start as you will have already identified the key points from the lessons you need to use for your revision.*

You will need to decide what format you would like your notes to be in. Here are some ideas.

Revision cards – physical

This is a very old-school method but it can still work well. You can:

* identify the key points from your lecture notes
* summarize these into a few lines on a card
* use diagrams, symbols or drawings to help you make mental links
* use them for self-testing – flip them over. Can you recall the information?

 You can buy revision cards with or without lines, and in a range of different colours. Use colour to code your topics and use different coloured pens in the same way. Match your coding to colours you have used throughout the year.

On the downside, it is sometimes difficult to keep cards in order and you may end up with huge wads of cards to carry around. I have seen students use hair bands to try and keep theirs together!

The limited size of the card has advantages as it means you have no choice but to be succinct. However, it can be frustrating if you are trying to link complex ideas when there simply isn't enough space on the card to show these connections. Card systems probably work best for subjects which are more objective rather than subjective.

An example from a student studying English language

Original source text to be condensed on to a card

Parts of speech are the basic grammatical categories that words can be classified into based on their function and role in a sentence. There are eight main parts of speech in English, each serving a specific purpose in constructing meaningful sentences. Understanding these parts of speech is crucial for developing effective communication skills and creating well-structured sentences. There are eight parts of speech: nouns, pronouns, verbs, adjectives, adverbs, prepositions, conjunctions and interjections.

Summarized on a revision note card

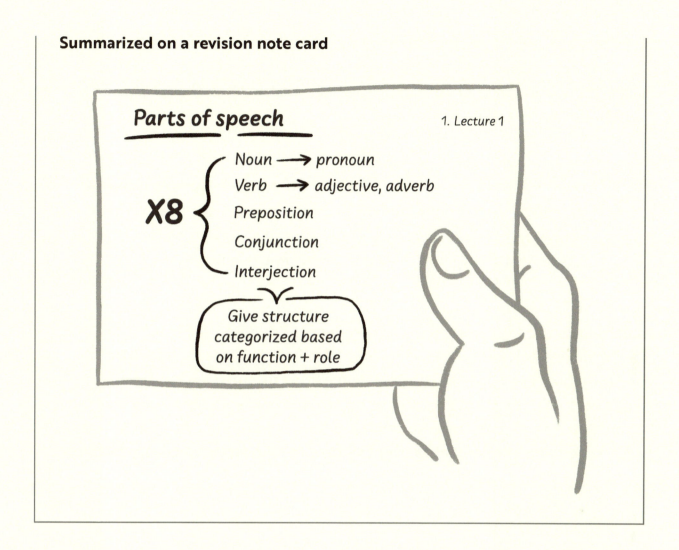

 Number your cards and put some kind of reference on them so that you can go back to your source if you need to check something. It also helps if you drop them!

Revision cards – digital

There are several digital options when it comes to making revision cards. The most common and straightforward ones I have encountered are Quizlet and Kahoot. You put your key points on to digital flashcards and create mini-quizzes for self-testing. Many students find them fun and interesting to use, particularly when you have to flip and match definitions.

They can work well if you find handwriting difficult or dislike making mistakes as it is definitely easier to keep things neat. However, some students find that using digital cards adds another layer of processing between their thoughts and the written word. This can be frustrating.

 There are many pre-existing subject-related quizzes on these websites, created by teachers and students. The quality of these can be variable. It is always best to make your own. The process of summarizing the information is a useful activity, even though it can be time consuming.

An alternative to the commercial card generators described above is the revision card maker called Anki, whose name originates from the Japanese word for memorization. This began as an open-source (free) resource but now offers paid upgrades too. This can be a helpful option to explore, particularly if you are studying an area where you need to revise and recall huge amounts of information. I have seen it used to particularly good effect by medical and foreign language students.

暗記する *Anki suru*

Memorization

An example of a student using Anki

Arthur, a medical student with ADHD, uses Anki to create revision cards. He enjoys the flexibility and the fact that it can hold decks of over 100,000 cards. Medical students have a lot of content to cover! He finds that Anki is very adaptable in terms of card layout choices and embedding media. There are also many open-source add-ons available, making it easy to customize. For example, he has added sound effects to indicate when he has passed or failed a quiz (a cheer or a scream). This is a good example of 'gamification' of studying, which works well for him.

Revision mind maps

These allow for freedom of thought and creativity and allow you to make 'big picture' links of ideas. Some students really enjoy being able to see how each part of their subject relates to the other. Have a look at the chapter on planning to see how mind maps can work, as they work almost exactly the same way for revision. You usually take the key points and expand the ideas from the centre. If you like to doodle or draw, you can also add some images to your revision maps. These don't replace the text but can help to reinforce your learning, as they enable your memory to make links between information. For example, if you are trying to remember a cycle or a process, you can draw arrows and images to indicate this. Equally, there isn't a rule that says your mind maps must look 'round' like a spider or a jellyfish. If it works better to have a mind map that progresses from left to right, for example, that's fine.

Flipchart paper allows you to make huge revision maps that you can stick up on your wall and refer to regularly. Wallpaper lining paper is an alternative option as it is much cheaper than flipchart paper. This works particularly well for historical timelines (adding images here can really help). You can also buy enormous sticky notes online, which work very well but are extremely expensive.

Revision/study groups

Revision/study groups can be very effective as long as they have a clear focus. It is best to gather a small group (three to four people is a good size) and meet regularly. This does rely on having good pre-existing relations with your peers and on enjoying social interaction. These are not for everyone.

> ### An example of a successful study group
>
> Four psychology students from a UK university decide to set up a study group to help them revise for the end-of-semester exam. Here are the steps they take:
>
> 1. Agree upon the most important revision areas (they checked this with their lecturer).
> 2. Divide these up among themselves.
> 3. Each student takes a topic, collates the material and produces a one-page factsheet about it.
> 4. Each student presents their summary factsheet at a meeting of the study group and gives copies to the others.
> 5. Students question each other and discuss the topic being presented.
> 6. Everyone takes a turn at this until all of the topics have been covered.
>
> This works so well because each student is learning about the subject in different ways, and there is lots of active questioning involved. This helps embed the information into their memories.

Using the idea of association to help you remember information

Generally, making some kind of mental link to help you remember tricky information is a good idea. It also helps if you can create visual images which are a bit out of the ordinary. This is a particularly useful strategy for dyslexic learners who may find it harder to associate a particular word with a concept.

Achieving Your Goals in Exams

> ### An example using association to help memory
>
> A trainee teacher has a pupil on her university school placement called Xertes, which is pronounced as if it starts with a 'Z'. The trainee teacher is dyslexic and is finding it hard to remember how to say or spell the pupil's name. She pictures her student jumping on top of the school's Xerox photocopier machine, which is something he would never do! Once she has made that link, she will never forget how to pronounce or spell it.

You can do something similar when you are revising. Use images or other associations to reinforce your learning. For example, perhaps you need to remember that Stephen Hawking was a famous cosmologist. You might picture a hawk swooping through a galaxy to help you remember his name and role.

 Remember that you can use your personal glossary to help you recall tricky words and that you can add images to it.

Method of loci (sometimes known as memory palaces)

 This takes the idea of making associations a stage further. It is an interesting theory which involves being able to both clearly visualize a familiar space **and** to mentally walk yourself through that space. This is important because you will be mentally 'attaching' the information you need to recall to certain objects/places within your familiar space. To retrieve the information in the exam, you will retrace your steps, walking back through the same space and 'collecting' the information from where you previously left it.

It is a bit of a love-it or hate-it strategy. Generally, I have found it works best for students who describe themselves as being creative and very visually aware. It is certainly worth experimenting with. This method works particularly well when you need to recall lists of facts such as historical events or scientific terms and names.

 You can also use this to help with your daily routines. For example, if you tend to leave home without your keys, books or phone, you might create a list of essential items and 'attach' these to a familiar space to help you remember them.

Here is a rather straightforward example, just to give you a feeling for how it can work.

Using the method of loci in practice

Paulo needs to remember a list of four key treaties which were signed at the end of the Second World War, known as the Paris Treaties of 1947. Here is his list:

1. Treaty of Peace with Italy
2. Treaty of Peace with Hungary
3. Treaty of Peace with Romania
4. Treaty of Peace with Finland.

Paulo chooses his kitchen as his familiar space. There are four treaties to remember, so he needs to choose four locations within his kitchen. This is how and **why** he chooses these locations:

Location	Attached information	Rationale
Coffee machine	Treaty of Peace with Italy	Paulo loves a cappuccino in the morning, and this makes him think of Italy.
Biscuit tin	Treaty of Peace with Hungary	Paulo is always snacking on biscuits when he is 'hungry' (I apologize for the pun).
Garlic	Treaty of Peace with Romania	Dracula came from Romania and he **hated** garlic.
Freezer	Treaty of Peace with Finland	Finland is cold and icy, like the freezer.

Can you see that the locations for attaching information are not just random? Paulo has made mental links between the words on his list and the locations. This will help him to remember.

For more complicated lists, you could try making a story. So, as you walk around your room, each item relates to another one. Here, perhaps the biscuit is dipped in the cappuccino and he is going to the freezer to gather ingredients to make a garlic-based meal.

Using mnemonics

Again, this does not work for everyone but can be particularly helpful for remembering ordered lists. Let's take the Paris Treaties example from earlier. Paulo still needs to remember a series of treaties for peace (poor Paulo). He might think of a short mnemonic sentence to help him remember their first letter and prompt him to recall their names:

Italy   I

Hungary   Hate

Romania   Rough

Finland   Feet

This also works because he really does hate rough feet, which strengthens the rather disgusting mental link for him!

 Try putting 'List of mnemonics' into an internet search engine. You will find ready-made lists of mnemonics to help you remember subject-related information, such as the periodic table, engineering and geographical terms.

Self-testing/practice-testing

This is one of the most effective ways of checking your own understanding and identifying any gaps in your knowledge. It can also help you to feel more secure in your own ability to retrieve information, which always helps with confidence when you are going into an exam.[6] You should aim to give yourself some kind of test at the end of each area you have covered. You could try using some online quiz resources to help with this (Quizlet, Kahoot or Anki).

Doing practice exam papers is also an excellent method of doing this. It is best to do these once you have **thoroughly** covered a topic at least once, or they can be a bit demotivating and unrealistic. There is also usually a limited number of papers available, so it's a good idea not to 'waste' the opportunity. Do the paper under timed conditions and then mark yourself. Keep a list of areas that you are weaker in and focus on these in your next revision session. If you just aren't 'getting' a particular topic, remember to ask your teacher or lecturer for help.

> *Many exams still require you to handwrite, so make sure you handwrite your practice papers. Being able to write legibly and quickly can really help you in exams, and we often get out of the habit of doing this.*

Summarizing and explaining aloud

You can also try summarizing your learning and then explaining it aloud. You can ask another person to listen to you, or you can record yourself using your phone. This is a slightly different way of testing your own knowledge which can also be effective as a study strategy. If you are explaining your topic to someone else, they could also question you about your knowledge, creating another method of testing.

How to approach exam questions

Different teachers will have different views on this, which I realize can be a bit confusing. That's because it's usually subject dependent. For example, sometimes you might be advised to do the last question first (if it is worth more marks and does not relate to the previous questions). However, this can be a really bad idea if the final question is building upon knowledge which has been explored earlier in the test! So, do listen to your tutors on this because they will know the exam system best.

Before the exam

It is always important to work out your timings and these are usually calculated using the number of available marks per question. Hopefully, you will have completed some practice papers, so **before** the exam, make sure you have worked out the time that you need to spend on each question. Your teachers can usually help you with this.

Here's an example:

English language examination: two hours (100 marks)		
Allow 10 minutes to check through the paper at the beginning and for reading and understanding questions throughout.		
Question	**Number of marks**	**Time to spend on it**
1	10	10 minutes
2	20	20 minutes
3	20	20 minutes
4	50	50 minutes
10 minutes at the end to check through work		

You will notice that the student has included some time at the start to read the question and some time at the end to check their work.

If you need to calculate the timings yourself the easiest way is to work out how much time you have per mark. This also allows you to 'knock off' some time for reading the paper (and questions as you go along) and for checking at the end.

Using the same example:

> The student has 120 minutes and 100 marks.
>
> They could calculate 120 divided by 100 to give them 1.2 minutes per mark.
>
> They can then multiply the marks for each question by 1.2 to give them the total number of minutes they have per question.
>
> **or**

> The student has 120 minutes and 100 marks.
>
> They will spend 10 minutes reading the paper (and the questions throughout) and 10 minutes checking at the end. That means they take 20 minutes off the total time for actually writing the paper.
>
> Their calculation is now 100 divided by 100, which gives them one minute per mark.

 It is a good idea to double-check that any accommodations or adjustments you are entitled to have been put in place. Send a quick email to the exams officer for your institution a day or two before your exam.

Arriving at the exam

When you arrive for your exam, take a minute or two to settle yourself:

* Take a deep breath.

* Check you have all of your equipment laid out on your desk.

* Once you are allowed to start, **read the instructions** carefully. Are there any compulsory questions? Are there some which have options? It is very easy to rush, misunderstand and lose lots of marks simply by omitting questions or doing the wrong question.

* Next, look through the entire paper. Just scan each page to get a feel for what is to come – this is not a detailed read. This is often calming and means that you are not shocked by what you see when you turn a page and find an unexpected diagram or image!

Starting to write

* First of all, jot down your timings, ideally on the exam paper next to each question (if you are allowed to write on the exam papers) or on a sheet of rough paper.

* Note down the actual time that you start each question, too, as this will help you to keep to your timing.

* Underline the keywords and phrases in the question, thinking about what they want you to demonstrate. This is your opportunity to **show** your subject knowledge.

* Decide what process they want you to complete. Are you critically analysing, discussing or explaining, etc.?

* Also, think about the content they want you to include and remember that they usually want you to explain **how, what and why**, not just describe.

 We know from Chapter 7, where we discussed understanding assignment questions, that we can use process verbs to help here.

Planning

In exams that are essay based, it is still important to plan your writing – honestly! Plans do not need to be very detailed, just a list of key points or a quick mind map. If you spend some time planning, you are less likely to get 'stuck' part-way through writing your answer, as you can refer back to your plan. If you are working through a more complicated question, you can tick off your plan as you go through it.

Remember that you are **showing** your learning. That means for maths and science questions you are usually required to show your workings too. It helps examiners understand how you reached your answer. Often you can get some marks for having sensible workings, even if your final answer is incorrect.

A note about take-home (open-book) exams

Increasingly, higher education students are being set take-home exams which are to be completed at home over a given period and submitted online within a deadline. Forty-eight hours seems to be a popular timeframe for these. This can feel very daunting, particularly as students are generally told they should not be spending more than a set number of hours on the exam within that period (usually around four). In my experience, this kind of 'flexible' timing is very difficult for neurodivergent students to deal with.

My best advice is to plan how you will manage your time in advance. So, create a time plan by dividing those exam days into 'study windows', incorporating lots of breaks and opportunities for some self-care, such as short walks and stretching. Do not expect to be able to work unrelentingly. When the exam is released, you can fill in the blanks in this plan, saying what part of the question/s you would like to do and when.

How you actually divide the question/s within your study windows is a very personal decision and will depend on many factors. The first is your subject and the type of questions you are given. Often, they seem to comprise a series of short-answer questions followed by a longer essay-type question. If that is the case, I would caution you not to spend all your time on the short answers to the detriment of the essay!

Also, you do not necessarily have to complete the questions in the order set, though do talk to tutors about this, just in case the order is relevant to your subject. For example, you might choose to do an 'easy' question first to get yourself warmed up.

Conversely, if you are feeling full of energy and eager to go, you could decide to do the trickiest question first. You should also think about how your energy levels fluctuate across a typical day and how this might affect your ability to think and write. It will influence the time of day that you decide to do the most difficult parts of your exam.

A final comment in this section – aim to submit your assignment at least two hours before the deadline. I have worked with several students who have struggled to upload their work on to university systems because their cohort is trying to do so at the same time. It's always best to assume that the technology will be flaky to avoid that horrible last-minute panic.

Getting stuck

I would wager that most people have experienced the horror of staring at a blank page and having absolutely no clue what to write. If that happens you can try the following:

* Take a few slow breaths to calm yourself.

* Lower your shoulders. Close your mouth gently and put the tip of your tongue gently behind your top teeth (this is a tip from my dentist for relaxing a jaw – I have no idea why it works, but it seems to).

* Do a chair push-up to help ground yourself and bring yourself back into your own body. Tuck your hands, palms down, underneath your outer thighs. You are now sitting on your hands which are between the back of your legs and the surface of the chair. Push your arms straight.

* Read the question again, more slowly.

Hopefully, that will work. If it doesn't, just move on to the next question. There is no point wasting time worrying about not being able to do it. You have left yourself time at the end which you can use to come back to that question if you need to.

 If you have reasonable adjustments or accommodations agreed upon for exams, these will almost certainly include breaks. You can use one of these to give yourself time to calm, regroup and be ready to go again.

There is only one more chapter left for you to read! We've looked mainly at writing so far, but lots of students also have a speaking and listening element to their courses. That means our final chapter will focus on oral skills, which includes giving presentations.

 Let's recap

In this chapter we have covered:

- reasonable adjustments
- importance of equity
- revision planning
- creating a list of topics
- putting topics into a detailed timetable
- interleaving topics
- breaking topics into daily tasks
- time management
- revision methods
- how to approach exam questions
- arriving at the exam
- starting to write
- planning
- getting stuck.

> **Key takeaway points from this chapter**
>
> - Your wellbeing comes first.
>
> - Ask for help and ensure you are getting the reasonable adjustments you are entitled to.
>
> - Mix your revision methods and stagger your revision so that you are interleaving topics.
>
> - Try and cover everything more than once, using different methods.

Chapter 9

ORAL SKILLS

Many courses have an element of oracy skills assessment, whether that is giving a presentation, participating in a Q&A discussion or being examined on your foreign language ability. These can be very daunting, so please keep the following in mind:

* There are **very** few people who are comfortable in these kinds of situations. Some will act as if they are, but they are really just being like a swan: calm on the surface but paddling like mad underneath!

* You are not expected to be perfect. The normal stutters and stumbles of conversation are absolutely fine.

* Remember that your teacher or tutor wants you to do well and they are on your side.

You may well be entitled to reasonable adjustments (accommodations) related to your neurodivergence. You can check this with your educational institution. For example, sometimes students who are very worried about presenting to groups may be able to present to their tutor alone or complete a recorded, narrated slide show instead.

Giving presentations

Often, advice given for this is quite general and lazily based on a neurotypical idea of what a good presentation will look like, particularly when it comes to body language. For example, you might be told to make eye contact with everyone in the room, not to move around too much, or fidget. This can add to the stress that you may already be feeling. I repeat my advice that it would be sensible to remind your teachers about your neurodivergence so that they put in place reasonable adjustments and also adapt their marking accordingly.

Let's start with some key tips:

* Know your subject. Make sure you have read the source material carefully and understand the topic. This will make you feel much more comfortable.

* Use notes. This will help keep you on track and reduce some of the cognitive load on your working memory. Make some brief notes which relate to your slides; you can include prompts and keywords to remind yourself what you want to say. You can use cue cards or you can print slide pages to write your ideas alongside.

* If you can manage it, try not to write a script to read aloud from. That's because it can throw you off if someone asks you a question and interrupts your flow. It can be very hard to find your place in your script and start again. It can also make a presentation feel very 'stiff' and reduce how easy you are to understand. However, if you feel this is the only way you will be able to do it, then please tell your teachers.

* Do not feel pressurized to keep eye contact if this is an issue for you. You should not have to feign neurotypical behaviour. However, sometimes students tell me that they wish they could keep eye contact, and we could have a whole other conversation about how we can internalize what is 'expected' of us, even when we know it feels entirely wrong! That said, if you do **want** to do this, you could look at people's foreheads or try to 'sweep' the room so that it seems you are giving attention to everyone. That means looking towards different parts of the room, not looking directly at individuals.

* Practice, practice, practice. You can do this in front of someone else, or you can record yourself. PowerPoint has an in-built function for narrating over slides. The other alternative is to just use your phone to record yourself.

* If you need to move around or fiddle with something, then so be it. The only thing I would say is to try and choose something quiet, like a piece of sticky-tac.

* Sometimes students feel a bit physically wobbly through nerves. If you have a case of jelly legs you could try holding on to the edge of a table or the back of a chair to help yourself feel a bit more 'grounded' and stable.

* Be kind to yourself. If you know that giving presentations feels stressful, build in some time for self-care. In the days before a presentation, you could make extra sure that you are having regular breaks and are remembering to eat and drink well. Perhaps after you have given your presentation you could plan to go home and cosy up in front of a familiar film, or have a head-clearing walk somewhere nice.

Structuring a presentation

This is very similar to how we structure any kind of interaction, so it needs a clear beginning, middle and end. This is so that your audience understands where they are going and doesn't feel lost. We can add signposting phrases along the way (just as we do when we are writing) to help with this. Look back at Chapter 7 'Completing Assignments, Essays and Dissertations' if you would like a reminder of some useful signposting phrases.

Almost always, you will be presenting a slide show and talking your audience through that. A typical structure for a presentation looks like this:

1. title page (overarching topic to be discussed)

2. aims or objectives (a list of what you will be covering)

3. contents slides (usually several)

4. conclusion (restating what has been covered, inviting any questions).

Aims or objectives

It doesn't really matter what you call this slide. Sometimes students use an opening phrase saying 'Today we will be covering…'

Include a bullet point list of the areas that you will be discussing during your presentation. Do not include details. You can read this list to them as it is succinct. In addition, you should:

* tell them how long you expect your presentation to last
* tell them whether you will be taking questions throughout, or at the end
* signpost the next slide: 'So, let's move on to look at…'

Contents slides

You are likely to have several of these. Generally, they should do the following:

* Be clearly titled. Titles will usually match those listed on your aims or objectives slide.
* Be succinct. Use bullet points and brief phrases.
* Be clear. Use a consistent design and a clear font, which is a decent size so it is easy to read. An off-white or pastel background generally reduces glare.
* Use formal English.
* Avoid using graphic effects, such as titles or images which appear from the edge of the screen. These detract from your message.
* Use images and diagrams carefully. These should always support your text, not dominate it. Choose them well and be aware of copyright issues. You can also add an image description (using alt text), which will make your slides accessible to visually impaired people.
* Be referenced. You will need to check this with your school or college, but certainly, at higher levels, you will be expected to have a reference page at the end to show the sources of your material and images.

Tell them the following:

* **About** the slide contents. Try not to read verbatim from every slide if you can – they have bullet points to prompt your thinking. Refer to your notes and expand by giving examples and making meaningful additional comments for your audience.

* Signpost each following slide as you move through the contents. For example, you might say something like 'Right, so now we understand the importance of this, we can move on to look at...'

 If you want to ask your audience questions during your presentation and are worried about remembering them, you can add them to your slides in a speech bubble. This not only helps you to remember but it gives your audience a chance to think about their response while you are speaking about the slide contents.

Conclusion

Your concluding slide is an opportunity to sum up your key points and to invite any questions. Do not include any new information in your conclusion. It will usually repeat the information on your first slide and say something like 'Today we have covered:...'

 Even the best-prepared person will be asked questions they do not know the answer to. Just be honest and say 'I do not know the answer to that right now, but I will find that out and get back to you.'

Oral examinations and Q&A discussions

Many subjects have an oral examination element, particularly modern foreign languages. There is an increasing emphasis on oracy in English language teaching too. Some qualifications require students to discuss their work in a 'question and answer' format with a tutor. Each of these scenarios will have different formats so you must understand the criteria under which you are being assessed. Ensure you are entirely clear. If you are not, you should check with your teacher/tutor.

Practice and preparation are always key. This is not always straightforward, as you do not always know the questions you will be asked beforehand. However, you will almost certainly know the type of questions you will be asked:

* Try to use past exam papers or the experiences of your teachers to help you come up with a list of likely questions or topics.

* Ideally, you should practise asking and answering questions with a peer. If you are uncomfortable with this, you can record yourself answering written questions.

* Remember to listen back so that you can check your grammar and vocabulary.

Tips for staying calm when giving presentations or during oral exams and discussions

* Try to slow down. Almost everyone talks too fast when they are under pressure (me included). Breathe between points. Pauses are fine.

* Take a second to relax your stance. Try standing with your legs slightly apart, bringing your shoulders down. If you are sitting, push your back into the chair and bring your shoulders back and down.

* If you stumble over your words do not worry. Just start your point again.

I hope this chapter has provided some useful advice if you have to give presentations or complete oral exams as part of your studies. I would like to return to my initial comments – it's very normal to feel nervous but remember that you are probably entitled to some adjustments because of your neurodivergence. Do ask your lecturers, teachers or person in charge of 'additional needs' if you are at all worried about using your oral skills.

 Let's recap

In this chapter we have covered:

- tips for giving presentations
- how to structure a presentation
- oral exams and Q&A discussions.

 Key takeaway points from this chapter

- Oral assessments are stressful and educators understand that.
- Check that you are getting the reasonable adjustments you are entitled to.
- You are not expected to be word perfect.
- Prepare well, so that you know your subject.
- Breathe; your tutors are on your side!

CONCLUSION

We have packed quite a lot into a not-very-big book! I hope that it has given you some food for thought. Perhaps it has made you think a bit about how you learn and has given you a better understanding of how you can play to your strengths, as well as giving you some tips about how you can approach areas of study skills that you find more challenging.

Most importantly, I hope that you have found some practical strategies that you can use to make your 'life in education' easier. I return to my advice at the very start, which is to keep experimenting until you find methods which suit you — this is definitely not a one-size-fits-all situation. Remember that you can also apply some of the strategies included in this book to your wider life, particularly those around personal organization.

You will find below a list of useful sources of further advice and information, which have all been used by students of mine over the years. They are internet-based, so should be accessible wherever you are in the world reading this guide. There's a glossary of terms too, which you might find helpful.

Before I let you go and get on with your work, I would like to sincerely thank you for taking the time to read and digest this book and I wish you every success in your studies and your future, wherever that may take you.

Finally, if you would like to tell me about things you find helpful or to suggest improvements, you can find me on Bluesky or X — just search using my name.

Happy studying!

Julia

USEFUL SOURCES

adhdfoundation.org.uk
Despite its title, this charity considers neurodiversity in the round, so also lists autism, dyslexia, DCD, dyscalculia, OCD and Tourette's as falling within its scope. It takes a positive view of neurodiversity and aims to support individuals to play to their strengths while acknowledging the challenges that differences can bring.

autisticgirlsnetwork.org
This is a small charity focused on autism in women and girls. Lots of my students find their content very helpful.

additudemag.com
An online magazine focused on all things ADHD (and overlapping neurodivergent conditions). Information is presented in an easily digestible format and many of my students enjoy reading their articles.

autismunderstood.co.uk
A website about autism for autistic young people, created by autistic people, from the charity Spectrum Gaming. It has lots of useful information about autism and information is presented in clear, 'bite-sized' chunks. It can be helpful for both autistic people themselves and their wider families in terms of raising their knowledge of autism.

bdadyslexia.org.uk
This is the website for the British Dyslexia Association. They have lots of useful resources including advice pages for children, adults, educators and employers. They also have some information and resources relating to dyscalculia.

embrace-autism.com
Founded by two autistic women, this autism-positive website provides accessible information about autism based on research findings.

fndaction.org.uk
This charity was founded by individuals with functional neurological disorder (FND) and supports people who are diagnosed with FND. They aim to raise awareness and improve access to health services.

hypermobility.org
This is the website for the Hypermobility Syndromes Association who support people with symptomatic hypermobility.

movementmattersuk.org
This website is focused on research related to dyspraxia/DCD. It presents information in an accessible, understandable format.

pdasociety.org.uk
This is the Pathological Demand Avoidance Society, a UK-based charity which works to support children and adults diagnosed with PDA.

@PurpleElla (YouTube)
Ella is an autism and ADHD advocate and vlogger. There is quite a bit of content related to anxiety and overwhelm which some students can find helpful.

Sedsconnective.org
A community-led charity supporting people who have symptomatic hypermobility (that means their hypermobility is causing them pain and/or functional difficulties) and are neurodivergent.

Tourettes-action.org.uk
A charity offering practical support as well as promoting research for people and families with Tourette's.

GLOSSARY

This glossary is necessarily brief and I've had to generalize to an extent. That's something which I try to avoid when I'm working with students! So, please know that individuals experience their neurodivergence differently. If you are particularly interested in one of the areas listed, I would encourage you to do some further reading and research, perhaps using the skills we have covered in this book.

Alexithymia
This term is used to describe when people have trouble understanding, recognizing and expressing their own emotions. It can mean that people either 'miss' the bodily clues that tell them about how they are feeling or can become confused about the meanings of these. For example, they might find it hard to differentiate between hunger and tiredness.

Autism
It's difficult to generalize because each autistic person is unique and their autism will affect them in different ways and to varying extents. Autism leads to differences in the ways that people communicate with others and interact with the world around them. This can result in challenges and difficulties as the world is 'configured' for neurotypical people. Autistic people can also have a wide range of strengths, including excellent problem-solving skills and attention to detail.

Attention deficit hyperactivity disorder (ADHD)
This condition impacts the way people behave. There are three types of ADHD which are currently diagnosed: inattentive type, hyperactive-impulsive type and combined type. The combined type is the most common. If someone has ADHD, they might find it hard to concentrate or difficult to stay still. They may have trouble organizing themselves or act on impulse. They might also have excellent social skills and be very creative.

Artificial intelligence (AI)
AI is a form of computer science. This technology can process huge amounts of data, recognize patterns and simulate human-like processes. In this context, it is used to describe natural language processing models which are systems able to generate human-like text.

Behavioural optometrists
These are opticians who aren't just focused on the ability to actually see, but on how this affects people in practice and different contexts. For example, they will think about whether someone sees comfortably when they are looking at a computer, reading or driving.

Bigger picture thinking
An ability to see the wider implications of an idea or course of action. This describes how some people look at long-term consequences rather than just focusing on small details.

Body-doubling
A study strategy which uses the idea of 'mirroring', so working alongside others who are completing similar tasks. This can help with focus and attention.

Burnout
This describes when a person has become so physically and emotionally overwhelmed that they are no longer able to function with day-to-day activities. It is the result of accumulated stress, fatigue and anxiety.

Cognitive load
How much our working memories are processing at a point in time.

Confirmation bias
When we look for sources or information which support our own view, as well as interpreting and analysing information in a way that tends to agree with our pre-existing ideas.

Developmental coordination disorder) (DCD)
Also known as dyspraxia. This affects physical coordination. It can impact balance and a person's understanding of their sense of space. They might seem clumsy. It can also impact smaller movements like tying shoelaces. People with DCD can be creative and socially aware.

Diagnostic assessment
Usually carried out by a medical specialist or sometimes a specialist teacher (in the case of specific learning difficulties like dyslexia). These use standardized tests to assess whether people meet predetermined criteria to be diagnosed with a given condition.

Disclosure
In this context, disclosure means telling someone about your neurodivergence. Sometimes you are asked to disclose this information when you register at college or university. Some organizations will collect this data for their equality, diversity and inclusion statistics. Some use it more proactively and will contact you to see if you would like additional support.

Dyscalculia
A difficulty in understanding numbers and the concept of numbers: problems with making sense of numbers, seeing patterns in numbers, ordering, estimating and calculating. Dyscalculic people can be creative and innovative.

Dysgraphia
The affects skills related to writing and the fine motor skills that are needed to write. It is often found in combination with dyslexia and dyspraxia.

Dyslexia
This affects skills around being able to read and spell. It can make it difficult to understand

the difference between the 'sounds' in words. This means it can be tricky to process verbal information quickly or to retain that information. Many dyslexic people are creative, with good oral skills.

Dyspraxia
Also known as DCD. This affects physical coordination. It can impact balance and a person's understanding of their sense of space. They might seem clumsy. It can also impact smaller movements like tying shoelaces. Dyspraxic people can be creative and socially aware.

Ehlers-Danlos syndromes (EDS)
These syndromes affect the body's connective tissues. Connective tissue supports other tissues and organs within the body. In EDS, these are often fragile and stretchy. There are 13 different types. The type referred to in this book is hypermobile EDS. This is thought to be the most common.

Energy accounting
A way of managing your energy levels by keeping track of things that reduce your energy or increase your energy.

Equality
Providing the same to everyone, regardless of any individual differences. For example, in a study skills context, this means that everyone gets to sit a two-hour exam to test their knowledge at the end of the year.

Equity
This is about justice and fairness. It recognizes that not everyone starts from the same point, so we can make changes to try and correct any imbalances. In a study skills context, it means making reasonable adjustments so that everyone has an equitable chance of success, for example, providing extra time for exams.

Executive functioning
This is an umbrella term for a set of memory-related skills that we use when we need to complete tasks. They include things like planning, attention and multitasking.

Functional neurological disorder (FND)
This causes problems with the way that the brain processes and sends signals throughout your body. It has wide-ranging symptoms but can include issues with limb control or weakness, and seizures. This can also result in pain or fatigue.

Hyper-focus
When you can focus intently on an activity for a prolonged period. This will be something you find fascinating. It might be a subject you love or another kind of leisure activity.

Hypermobility
This is a medical condition which refers to an unusually wide range of movement in joint/s. Some people with hypermobility have pain; others do not.

Interoception
This is our sense of what is happening inside our own bodies. It tells us when we are hungry, thirsty or ill. It also helps us to understand our emotions.

Ishikawa diagram
Also known as a fishbone diagram (because of its shape) which was developed as a strategic business problem-solving tool. Creating an Ishikawa diagram helps you to visually represent a problem by showing causes and effects.

Long-term knowledge systems
This is the part of your memory system where you hold information that needs to be stored. You can recall this when you want to (most of the time).

Masking
'Masking' is a phrase which is often used, particularly by people in the autistic community, to describe how they have learned that they must appear to be neurotypical in social situations to 'fit in' better. Sometimes this is deliberate and sometimes it is more subconsciously learned behaviour. People with other neurodivergent conditions may also mask.

Meares-Irlen syndrome
This is the name given to a form of visual stress which causes difficulties with reading. It is not related to the function of the eyes themselves, but to how the brain can process visual input.

Meltdown
This is an expression of mental and/or physical distress which results from being overwhelmed. It leads to a loss of control over emotions and agitation. People in meltdown are in a state of high anxiety and/or fear, though they may appear angry or aggressive. This is not a feature of neurodivergence per se but the result of an unmanageable amount of distress.

Metacognition
Thinking about your own learning and thought processes. You can use this to help analyse what works for you and what doesn't when you are studying.

Mirroring
Also known as 'body-doubling'. This strategy involves working alongside others who are completing similar tasks. This can help with focus and attention.

Monotropism
A way of thinking that means attention is pulled more intensely towards a narrow range of interests. This is sometimes described as being a bit like being in a tunnel. It can be hard to see outside this tunnel.

Mnemonic
A way of remembering something most often by using a pattern of letters. For example, 'Richard of York gave battle in vain' is a very common one to help remember the colours of the rainbow: red, orange, yellow, green, blue, indigo, violet.

Neurodiversity
A term which describes the diversity which exists across all people in terms of brain function and behavioural traits.

Neurodivergent
People who differ from what is considered to be the 'norm' concerning their brain function and behavioural traits.

Neurotypical
People who are considered to be the 'norm' in terms of their brain function and behavioural traits.

Overwhelm
A feeling which is usually the result of too much 'incoming' into a neurodivergent brain and body. This can be due to information overload, a reaction to unexpected change and sensory or emotional input. It can lead to shutdowns or meltdowns. This is not intrinsic to neurodivergence per se but rather a response to overwhelming stimuli.

Glossary

Pacing
Pacing strategies help you to find a rhythm or routine of studying/being that means you are not overdoing it or underdoing it, finding a level that is sustainable both emotionally and physically.

Pathological demand avoidance (PDA)
Sometimes a feature in neurodivergent profiles, this behaviour is often perceived as being oppositional towards complying with requests and expectations made by others. This is founded on feelings of anxiety and pressure.

Proprioception
A term to describe our understanding of our own bodies within space. It's how we know where our body parts are concerning each other and other objects. People with poor proprioception might find it difficult not to bump into things or to judge how hard to pull or push things.

Qualitative research
This kind of research is descriptive. It requires collecting non-numerical data to gain an understanding of how people feel, think or behave (usually concerning others) within certain contexts.

Quantitative research
This kind of research requires collecting and analysing statistical (numerical) data to find trends, relationships and insights into a problem.

Reasonable adjustments
Sometimes known as accommodations, these are changes which are made to remove or reduce a disadvantage related to someone's neurodivergence. This could include extra time for exams, allowing the use of headphones in class, providing extra breaks etc.

Rejective sensitive dysphoria
Feeling overwhelming emotional pain in response to feelings of failure or rejection.

Shutdown
A response to feeling overwhelmed and a reaction to mental and/or physical distress. This can feel like being unable to mentally process at all. Some people are unable to communicate when this has happened to them.

Speech, language and communication needs (SLCN)
A term which describes a wide range of challenges that an individual might face in relation to how they communicate. This can apply to how they can understand others, as well as how they can express themselves.

Specific learning difficulty (SpLD)
This affects particular aspects of learning. It is not the same as having a learning disability. Examples of specific learning difficulties are dyslexia, dyspraxia, dysgraphia and dyscalculia.

SWOT analysis
This stands for strengths, weaknesses, opportunities and threats. It is a decision-making tool, originally intended for business use. It helps you to take a 'snapshot' of a moment in time and try to work out what is most important to you.

Theory of loci
A memory technique which involves thinking about a very familiar place and 'attaching' the information you need to remember to spots within that place.

Thesis statement
This is a sentence which sets out your position at a glance. It's included in your introduction and sets out your standpoint or argument.

Tourette's (Tourette syndrome)
This condition causes a person to have involuntary movements and sounds. These are called tics. These can be very tiring and distressing.

Visual stress
This makes reading difficult and uncomfortable. It can cause text to blur, wobble or move. Some people can experience glare from paper and screens. It can be hard to follow lines of text. Sometimes it may also make it hard to judge distance on stairs and escalators. This is usually unrelated to the physical operation of the eye itself but an issue with how the brain processes incoming information.

Working memory
The way in which our brains can hold a small amount of information and then perform other operations on that information. For example, being given two numbers and adding them together is using our working memory. Often, for neurodivergent people, working memory can become overloaded if there is too much information coming in at once.

ENDNOTES

Introduction

1   Charlton, J.I. (1998) *Nothing About Us Without Us: Disability Oppression and Empowerment*, 1st edition. Oakland, California: University of California Press. Available at: www.jstor.org/stable/10.1525/j.ctt1pnqn9 (Accessed: 26/04/2025)

2   www.psychologytoday.com/gb/basics/executive-function (Accessed: 26/04/2025)

3   Dijkhuis, R., De Sonneville, L., Ziermans, T., Staal,W. and Swaab, H. (2020) 'Autism symptoms, executive functioning and academic progress in higher education students.' *Journal of Autism and Developmental Disorders*, 50(4), pp. 1353–1363. Available at: https://link.springer.com/article/10.1007/s10803-019-04267-8 (Accessed: 22/11/2024)

4   Singer, J. (1998, 2016) *Neurodiversity: The Birth of an Idea*. London: Judy Singer.

5   Asasumasu, K. (2023) Kassiane Asasumasu on Neurodivergent #shorts, *Foundations for Divergent Minds*. Available at: www.youtube.com/watch?v=J0BP5nbgdu4 (Accessed: 03/04/2024)

6   Yao, Y. (2024) 'Can we mitigate AI's environmental impacts?' *Yale School of the Environment.* 10 October. Available at: https://environment.yale.edu/news/article/can-we-mitigate-ais-environmental-impacts#:~:text=Artificial%20intelligence%20(AI)%20is%20powered,biggest%20contributor%20to%20global%20warming (Accessed: 25/11/2024)

Chapter 1

1   Bjork, R.A., Dunlosky, J. and Kornell, N. (2013) 'Self-regulated learning: beliefs, techniques, and illusions.' *Annual Review of Psychology*, 64(1), pp. 417–444. Available at: https://doi.org/10.1146/annurev-psych-113011-143823 (Accessed: 07/08/2023)

2   Adapted from: Baddley, A. (2000) 'The episodic buffer: a new component of working memory?' *Trends in Cognitive Sciences*, 4(11), pp. 417–423. Available at: https://doi.org/10.1016/S1364-6613(00)01538-2 (Accessed: 07/08/2023)

3   Bjork, R.A., Dunlosky, J. and Kornell, N. (2013) 'Self-regulated learning: beliefs, techniques, and illusions.' *Annual Review of Psychology*, 64(1), pp. 417–444. Available at: https://doi.org/10.1146/annurev-psych-113011-143823 (Accessed: 07/08/2023)

Chapter 2

1   Bernal-Morales, B. and Bernal-Morales, B. (2018) *Health and Academic Achievement.* Edited by B. Bernal-Morales. London, England: IntechOpen. Available at: https://doi.org/10.5772/intechopen.68719 (Accessed: 03/07/2023)

2   Hobbs, C., Jelbert, S., Santos, L.R. and Hood, B. (2024) 'Long-term analysis of a psychoeducational course on university students' mental well-being.' *Higher Education*, 88, pp. 2093–2105. Available at: https://doi.org/10.1007/s10734-024-01202-4 (Accessed 01/05/2024)

3   Hobbs, C., Jelbert, S., Santos, L.R. and Hood, B. (2024) 'Long-term analysis of a psychoeducational course on university students' mental well-being.' *Higher Education*, 88, pp. 2093–2105. Available at: https://doi.org/10.1007/s10734-024-01202-4 (Accessed 01/05/2024)

4   Meaux, J.B. and Chelonis, J.J. (2003) 'Time perception differences in children with and without ADHD.' *Journal of Pediatric Health Care*, 17(2), pp. 64–71. Available at: https://doi.org/10.1067/mph.2003.26 (Accessed: 24/09/2023)

5   Brewer, R., Cook, R. and Bird, G. (2016) 'Alexithymia: a general deficit of interoception.' *Royal Society Open Science*, 3(10), pp. 150664–150664. Available at: https://doi.org/10.1098/rsos.150664 (Accessed: 02/03/2024)

6   Kinnaird, E., Stewart, C. and Tchanturia, K. (2019) 'Investigating alexithymia in autism: a systematic review and meta-analysis.' *European Psychiatry*, 55, pp. 80–89. Available at: https://doi.org/10.1016/j.eurpsy.2018.09.004 (Accessed: 12/04/2024)

7   Accardo, A.L., Pontes, N.M.H. and Pontes, M.C.F. (2024) 'Heightened anxiety and depression among autistic adolescents with ADHD: findings from the National Survey of Children's Health 2016-2019.' *Journal of Autism and Developmental disorders*, 54(2), pp. 563–576. Available at: https://doi.org/10.1007/s10803-022-05803-9 (Accessed: 11/11/2023)

8   Chapman, L., Rose, K., Hull, L. and Mandy, W. (2022) '"I want to fit in… but I don't want to change myself fundamentally": a qualitative exploration of the relationship between masking and mental health for autistic teenagers.' *Research in Autism Spectrum Disorders*, 99, article 102069. Available at: https://doi.org/10.1016/j.rasd.2022.102069 (Accessed: 02/03/2024)

9   Bedrossian, L. (2021) 'Understand and address complexities of rejection sensitive dysphoria in students with ADHD.' *Disability Compliance for Higher Education*, 26(10), p. 4. Available at: https://doi.org/10.1002/dhe.31047 (Accessed: 01/10/2023)

10   Kildahl, A.N., Helverschou, S.B., Rysstad, A.L., Wigaard, E., Hellerud, J.M.E. and Howlin, P. (2021) 'Pathological demand avoidance in children and adolescents: a systematic review.' *Autism*, 25(8), pp. 2162–2176. Available at: https://doi.org/10.1177/13623613211034382 (Accessed: 02/02/2024)

11   Goeta, D. and Demartini, B. (2023) 'Clinical overlap between functional neurological disorders

and autism spectrum disorders: a preliminary study.' *European Psychiatry*, 66(S1), p. S336. Available at: https://doi.org/10.1192/j.eurpsy.2023.736 (Accessed: 12/02/2023)

12   Nisticò, V., Iacono, A., Goeta, D., Tedesco, R., Giordano, B., Faggioli, R. *et al.* (2022) 'Hypermobile spectrum disorders symptoms in patients with functional neurological disorders and autism spectrum disorders: a preliminary study.' *Frontiers in Psychiatry*, 13, article 943098. Available at: https://doi.org/10.3389/fpsyt.2022.943098 (Accessed: 04/04/2024)

13   Royal College of Speech and Language Therapists (2023) *What Are Speech, Language and Communication Needs?* Available at: www.rcslt.org/wp-content/uploads/media/Project/RCSLT/rcslt-communication-needs-factsheet.pdf (Accessed 14/05/2024)

14   Donaghy, B., Moore, D. and Green, J. (2023) 'Co-occurring physical health challenges in neurodivergent children and young people: a topical review and recommendation.' *Child Care in Practice*, 29(1), pp. 3–21. Available at: https://doi.org/10.1080/13575279.2022.2149471 (Accessed: 12/11/2023)

15   Casanova, E.L., Baeza-Velasco, C., Buchanan, C.B. and Casanova, M.F. (2020) 'The relationship between autism and Ehlers-Danlos syndromes/hypermobility spectrum disorders.' *Journal of Personalized Medicine*, 10(4), p. 260. Available at: https://doi.org/10.3390/jpm10040260 (Accessed: 02/03/2024)

16   Miserandino, C. (2003) *The Spoon Theory*. Available at: www.butyoudontlooksick.com (Accessed: 12/12/2023)

17   Shen, C., Qiang, L., Chamberlain, S.R., Morgan, S., Romero-Garcia, R., Du, J. *et al.* (2020) 'What is the link between attention-deficit/hyperactivity disorder and sleep disturbance? A multimodal examination of longitudinal relationships and brain structure using large-scale population-based cohorts.' *Biological Psychiatry (1969)*, 88(6), pp. 459–469. Available at: https://doi.org/10.1016/j.biopsych.2020.03.010 (Accessed: 03/03/2024)

18   Shen, C., Qiang, L., Chamberlain, S.R., Morgan, S., Romero-Garcia, R., Du, J. *et al.* (2020) 'What is the link between attention-deficit/hyperactivity disorder and sleep disturbance? A multimodal examination of longitudinal relationships and brain structure using large-scale population-based cohorts.' *Biological Psychiatry (1969)*, 88(6), pp. 459–469. Available at: https://doi.org/10.1016/j.biopsych.2020.03.010 (Accessed: 03/03/2024)

19   BDA The Association of UK Dieticians (2023) *Diet, Behaviour and Learning in Children*. Available at: www.bda.uk.com/resource/diet-behaviour-and-learning-children.html#:~:text=Eating%20a%20wide%20variety%20of,supplements%20may%20help%20some%20children (Accessed: 03/09/2023)

20   Perini, R., Bortoletto, M., Capogrosso, M., Fertonani, A. and Miniussi, C. (2016) 'Acute effects of aerobic exercise promote learning.' *Scientific Reports*, 6(1), article 25440. Available at: https://doi.org/10.1038/srep25440 (Accessed: 18/09/2023)

21   Sng, E., Frith, E. and Loprinzi, P.D. (2018) 'Temporal effects of acute walking exercise on learning and memory function.' *American Journal of Health Promotion*, 32(7), pp. 1518–1525. Available at: https://doi.org/10.1177/0890117117749476 (Accessed: 13/12/2023)

22 Lane A.M. and Lovejoy D.J. (2001) 'The effects of exercise on mood changes: the moderating effect of depressed mood.' *Journal of Sports Medicine and Physical Fitness*, 41(4), pp. 539–545. Available at: https://pubmed.ncbi.nlm.nih.gov/11687775/ (Accessed: 10/05/2024)

23 Nichols, W. (2014) *Blue Mind: The Surprising Science that Shows How Being Near, In, On, or Under Water Can Make You Happier, Healthier, More Connected, and Better at What You Do*. New York and London: Little, Brown & Co.

24 Shoemaker, L.N., Wilson, L.C., Samuel J.E., Machado, L., Thomas, K.N. and Cotter, J.D. (2019) 'Swimming-related effects on cerebrovascular and cognitive function.' *Physiological Reports*, 7(20), e14247. Available at: https://doi.org/10.14814/phy2.14247 (Accessed: 11/02/2025)

25 Milton, D.E.M. (2012) 'On the ontological status of autism: the "double empathy problem.' *Disability & Society*, 27(6), pp. 883–887. Available at: https://doi.org/10.1080/09687599.2012.710008 (Accessed: 04/04/2024)

26 Gov.UK (2024) *Disability Rights*. Available at: www.gov.uk/rights-disabled-person/education-rights (Accessed: 20/04/2024)

27 Bourdieu, P. (1977) *Outline of a Theory of Practice*. Translated by R. Nice. Cambridge: Cambridge University Press.

Chapter 3

1 Estrada-Tenorio, S., Julian, J., Aibar, A., Martin, J. and Saragoza, J. (2020) 'Academic achievement and physical activity: the ideal relationship to promote a healthier lifestyle in adolescents.' *Journal of Physical Activity & Health*, 17(5), pp. 525–532. Available at: https://doi.org/10.1123/jpah.2019–0320 (Accessed: 29/08/2023)

2 Bernal-Morales, B. and Bernal-Morales, B. (2018) *Health and Academic Achievement*. Edited by B. Bernal-Morales. London: IntechOpen. Available at: https://doi.org/10.5772/intechopen.68719 (Accessed: 03/07/2023)

3 Lakein, A. (1973) *How to Get Control of Your Time and Your Life*. New York, New York: New American Library.

4 The Noun Project. Available at: https://thenounproject.com (Accessed: 26/04/2025)

Chapter 4

1 Bensoussan, B.E. and Fleisher, C.S. (2008) *Analysis Without Paralysis : 10 Tools to Make Better Strategic Decisions*, 1st edition. Upper Saddle River, New Jersey: FT Press.

2 Project School Wellness (2023) *The D.E.C.I.D.E. Model: A Tool for Teaching Students How to Make Healthy Decisions*. Available at: www.projectschoolwellness.com/the-d-e-c-i-d-e-model-a-tool-for-teaching-students-how-to-making-healthy-decisions (Accessed: 15/04/2024)

3 Ishikawa, K. and Loftus, J.H. (1990) *Introduction to Quality Control*, vol. 98, p. 31. Tokyo: 3A Corporation.

4   Hasson, U. and Frith, C.D. (2016) 'Mirroring and beyond: coupled dynamics as a generalized framework for modelling social interactions.' *Philosophical Transactions of the Royal Society of London. Series B. Biological Sciences*, 371(1693), article 20150366. Available at: https://doi.org/10.1098/rstb.2015.0366 (Accessed: 09/09/2023)

5   Wilcox, K. (2023) 'How doodling helps kids with ADHD to focus.' *Psychology Today*. 18 April. Available at: www.psychologytoday.com/gb/blog/mythbusting-adhd/202304/how-doodling-helps-kids-with-adhd-to-focus (Accessed: 24/11/24)

Chapter 5

1   Pauk, W. and Owens, R. (2010) Chapter 10: 'The Cornell System: Take Effective Notes.' In *How to Study in College*, 10th edition. Boston, Massachusetts: Wadsworth.

2   The Learning Strategies Center (2023) *The Cornell Note Taking System*. Cornell University. Available at: https://lsc.cornell.edu/how-to-study/taking-notes/cornell-note-taking-system (Accessed: 09/09/2023)

3   Clark, E.G. and Davis, A.D. (1982) 'Note-making with T-Notes.' *Journal of Developmental and Remedial Education*, 5.

Chapter 6

1   Denton, T.F. and Meindl, J.N. (2016) 'The effect of colored overlays on reading fluency in individuals with dyslexia.' *Behavior Analysis in Practice*, 9(3), pp. 191–198. Available at: https://doi.org/10.1007/s40617-015-0079-7 (Accessed: 23/09/2023)

2   Ogle, D. (1986) 'K-W-L: a teaching model that develops active reading of expository text.' *The Reading Teacher*, 39, pp. 564–570. Available at: http://dx.doi.org/10.1598/RT.39.6.11 (Accessed: 01/12/2023)

3   Conan-Doyle, A. (1892) 'The Adventure of the Engineer's Thumb.' *The Strand Magazine*, London.

4   Robinson, F.P. (1941) *Effective Study*. New York: Harper and Row Publishers.

5   Asiri, A. and Momani, M. (2017) 'The effectiveness of using SQ3R to teach reading skills.' *Asian Journal of Educational Research*, 5, ISSN 2311–6080. Available at: www.multidisciplinaryjournals.com/wp-content/uploads/2017/01/FULL-PAPER-THE-EFFECTIVENESS-OF-USING-SQ3R-TO-TEACH-READING-SKILLS.pdf (Accessed: 10/11/2023)

Chapter 7

1   Kolb, D.A. (1984) *Experiential Learning: Experience as the Source of Learning Development*. Saddle River, New Jersey: Prentice Hall.

2   Kolb, D.A. (1984) *Experiential Learning: Experience as the Source of Learning Development*. Saddle River, New Jersey: Prentice Hall.

3   Conan-Doyle, A. (1921) 'The Adventure of the Mazarin Stone.' *The Strand Magazine*, London.

Chapter 8

1   Kang, S.H.K. (2016) 'Spaced repetition promotes efficient and effective learning: policy implications for instruction.' *Policy Insights from the Behavioral and Brain Sciences*, 3(1), pp. 12–19. Available at: https://doi.org/10.1177/2372732215624708 (Accessed: 11/09/2023)

2   Bjork, R.A., Dunlosky, J. and Kornell, N. (2013) 'Self-regulated learning: beliefs, techniques, and illusions.' *Annual Review of Psychology*, 64(1), pp. 417–444. Available at: https://doi.org/10.1146/annurev-psych-113011-143823 (Accessed: 07/08/2023)

3   Cirillo, F. (2018) *The Pomodoro Technique: The Acclaimed Time-Management System that Has Transformed How We Work.* New York, New York: Crown.

4   Dunlosky, J., Rawson, K.A., Marsh, E.J., Mitchell, J.N. and Willingham, D.T. (2013) 'Improving students' learning with effective learning techniques: promising directions from cognitive and educational psychology.' *Psychological Science in the Public Interest*, 14(1), pp. 4–58. Available at: https://doi.org/10.1177/1529100612453266 (Accessed: 23/08/2023)

5   Bjork, R.A., Dunlosky, J. and Kornell, N. (2013) 'Self-regulated learning: beliefs, techniques, and illusions.' *Annual Review of Psychology*, 64(1), pp. 417–444. Available at: https://doi.org/10.1146/annurev-psych-113011-143823 (Accessed: 07/08/2023)

6   Bjork, R.A., Dunlosky, J. and Kornell, N. (2013) 'Self-regulated learning: beliefs, techniques, and illusions.' *Annual Review of Psychology*, 64(1), pp. 417–444. Available at: https://doi.org/10.1146/annurev-psych-113011-143823 (Accessed: 07/08/2023)